How to
Sell Your House
in Tough Times

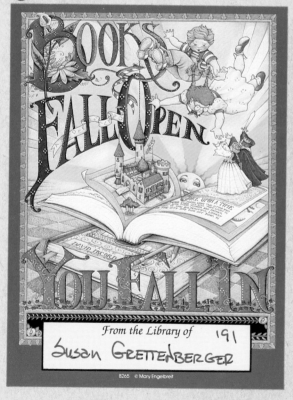

How to
Sell Your House
in Tough Times

PETER DAVIDSON

A PERIGEE BOOK

To Ken Horner and Jerry Stockdale for teaching me the real estate business, and to Ron Hickman for his never-ending encouragement.

—PETER DAVIDSON

Perigee Books
are published by
The Putnam Publishing Group
200 Madison Avenue
New York, NY 10016

Library of Congress Cataloging-in-Publication Data

Davidson, Peter, date.
How to sell your house in tough times / Peter Davidson.
p.   cm.
ISBN 0-399-51690-5 (trade pbk.)
1. House selling.   I. Title.
HD1379.D28   1991   91-12574   CIP
643′.12—dc20

Cover design by Terrence Fehr

Printed in the United States of America

1   2   3   4   5   6   7   8   9   10

Contents

Introduction

"Is it possible—can I really sell my own home without the aid of a real estate company?" This may be the question you are asking yourself right now. The answer is *Yes, you can*! And you can even do it in a "tough" real estate market, when homes are generally more difficult to sell.

This is not idle speculation. Many people from all over the country have sold their own homes. Sometimes it has been because of pure luck, other times it has been because of careful planning and design. The goal of *How to Sell Your House in Tough Times*, is to take the guesswork out of the process and provide you with easy-to-follow, step-by-step guidelines that actually work.

How to Sell Your House in Tough Times is a complete guide to everything you need to do from start to finish. It contains valuable information on how to prepare your home for sale, how to appraise it, advertise it, promote it, show it to prospects, and close the deal. Special attention is given to tactics that work in a tough market, so you will be able to sell your home even when other homes aren't selling.

Selling your home yourself and saving the real estate commission may be the easiest money you will ever earn; and you'll learn a lot in the process, derive a great feeling of personal satisfaction, and have fun all at the same time.

In short, it *can* be done. *You* can sell your own home, and it will be very worthwhile for you to do it. You'll be amazed at just how easy it is.

—Peter Davidson

1

The Ever-changing Real Estate Market

As the national economy and local conditions change, the real estate market likewise changes. Real estate prices, and the prospects of readily selling your home, increase in good times and decrease in bad times.

The real estate market is described as being "strong" or a "seller's market" when home sales are brisk and the demand for homes is high. It is described as being "tough," or "soft," or a "buyer's market" when there are more homes available for sale than there are active buyers.

The national economy affects the saleability of all homes nationwide. If employment is high, home loan interest rates are low, and an optimistic attitude about the future prevails, a strong overall real estate market will exist. On the other hand, if unemployment is high, interest rates on home loans are high, and a pessimistic attitude exists, the real estate market will be soft.

The real estate market is affected more directly by the

local economy in your community than by the national economy. For instance, if you live in a community of 100,000 people and an announcement has just been made that a major manufacturer will build a plant that will employ 10,000 workers, your economy will boom, regardless of the national economy. Likewise, if a plant employing 10,000 workers closes, your local economy and the real estate market will sag regardless of how strong the national economy and national real estate market may be.

The real estate market is ever-changing. If interest rates drop, say even as little as ½%, the market could heat up virtually overnight. Likewise, an increase in interest rates or a national crisis might slow down the market very quickly. Usually, however, except for fast-breaking local developments or noteworthy national news, the real estate market is slow to change from a strong to a tough market or from a tough market to a strong one.

During a "strong" market, you can expect your home to sell more rapidly and at a better price than during a "tough" market. But the home will not sell by itself. You will need to employ all of the techniques outlined in this book to ensure that your home sells as rapidly and at as high a price as possible. Your work will be easier in a strong market, but you must still pursue the sale of your home very aggressively.

Even in a tough market, homes do sell. People are still working and earning a living. People are getting promoted to new and better-paying jobs. People are being transferred from one community to another or are moving voluntarily. Babies are being born and families are outgrowing their present homes. Children are leaving home, and the "empty nest" parents no longer need nor want the large family home.

Yes, even in the worst of times, homes sell—millions

of them per year. Reflect for a moment on the 11-year period from 1978–1988. This era was filled with periods of boom and bust and everything in between. There were periods of inflation, recession, high interest rates, high unemployment, and about every economic disaster you can name. Yet, as shown in the following data taken from the *Statistical Abstract of the United States, 1990*, millions of homes still sold.

EXISTING ONE-FAMILY HOMES SOLD IN UNITED STATES

Year	No. Sold
1978	3,986,000
1979	3,827,000
1980	2,973,000
1981	2,419,000
1982	1,990,000
1983	2,719,000
1984	2,868,000
1985	3,214,000
1986	3,565,000
1987	3,526,000
1988	3,594,000

So, whether the real estate market is "strong" or "tough," homes sell. And, whether the real estate market is "strong" or "tough," you *can* sell your own home. Pay attention to national and local news to determine the status of the real estate market, and then apply the principles in this book accordingly.

2

Why Selling Your Own Home Makes (Dollars and) Sense

It is not the intention of this book to be critical of real estate companies and their salespeople. They do provide a useful service for many. It is this book's purpose, however, to aid and guide you so that you can do for yourself what you otherwise might hire a real estate company to do for you. In fact, there are two reasons why you can actually do this job *better* than a real estate company can.

First, you know your home better than anyone else. You know its advantages, special appeals, and attractions. After all—you bought the home, you have lived in it. No real estate salesperson, regardless of how conscientious, competent, or well-meaning they may be, will ever know your home as well as you know it yourself.

Second, it's the *only* home you are trying to sell. You

can devote your full attention and sales efforts to it alone. It's not just one of fifty, a hundred, or perhaps several hundred that the real estate company is trying to sell.

A common complaint of homeowners is that the real estate company they listed their home with just doesn't seem to work at it very hard: They don't show it to prospects, they don't advertise and promote it, and they don't keep the homeowner informed of what's happening, if anything. There may be some legitimate reasons for this, but often it's simply because your home is one of many the real estate company has responsibility for, and none of them receive much individual attention.

How Much Will You "Earn" For Your Efforts?

The rate of real estate commission varies from community to community and from agency to agency within any particular community. The rate also varies with the type of property being sold. Most real estate commissions range from 6% to 8% on residential properties. Often, the rate is 10% or higher on commercial properties, and may range from 3% to 6% on agricultural land.

The amount of real estate commission that you would be required to pay can be easily calculated by multiplying the sales price times the rate of commission as shown in the table on page 16.

As you can see, the amount of money you can "earn" by selling your own home is substantial.

Since the value of one's home is often indicative of a person's overall financial standing, a cash savings of $3,000 on the sale of a $50,000 home may mean as much to that homeowner as the $14,000 savings means to the owner of a $200,000 home.

Calculating Real Estate Commission

Sales Price	×	Rate of Commission	=	Amount of Commission
$ 25,000	×	6%	=	$ 1,500
25,000	×	7%	=	1,750
25,000	×	8%	=	2,000
50,000	×	6%	=	3,000
50,000	×	7%	=	3,500
50,000	×	8%	=	4,000
75,000	×	6%	=	4,500
75,000	×	7%	=	5,250
75,000	×	8%	=	6,000
100,000	×	6%	=	6,000
100,000	×	7%	=	7,000
100,000	×	8%	=	8,000
150,000	×	6%	=	9,000
150,000	×	7%	=	10,500
150,000	×	8%	=	12,000
200,000	×	6%	=	12,000
200,000	×	7%	=	14,000
200,000	×	8%	=	16,000
300,000	×	6%	=	18,000
300,000	×	7%	=	21,000
300,000	×	8%	=	24,000

If you wonder whether or not the amount of money you will save by selling your own home is worth the effort, you might ask yourself this question: "How long would it take me to accumulate in a savings account the $3,000, $5,000, or $15,000 I would pay a real estate company for selling my home for me?" Chances are, if you are an average individual, the answer is "A long, long time." A quick review of your present savings account balance and the length of time it took you to accumulate that amount will provide you with a good indication.

In addition to the money you'll earn by selling your own home, there are other important types of earnings. Certainly, the personal satisfaction you'll gain from "doing it yourself" should not be overlooked. Then, too, you will learn and grow from the experience. The knowledge you gain from selling your own home will make you a better buyer next time around and will probably even save you money on your next purchase.

All too often our lives can be uneventful, monotonous, and humdrum. Attacking an important project like selling your own home will add some spice and excitement to your life—you will find it to be great fun!

3

Getting Your Home Ready For Sale

Almost any home in any price range has a few imperfections that the owner is willing to live with. A cracked windowpane, a worn carpet, a smudge on the wall, a loose doorknob, a small crack in the ceiling, or a few weeds in the yard don't cause too much concern.

When it comes time to sell your home, however, these relatively small imperfections can loom like mountainous obstacles in a buyer's eyes. In general, buyers want to purchase a home that's in a good state of repair. The thought of replacing broken windows, painting dirty walls, shampooing carpets, varnishing woodwork, and fixing leaky faucets will drive a prospective buyer away—to a home that doesn't require so much of this work.

If the thought of doing all of that work to put the home into top-notch shape doesn't turn the buyer off, the uncertainty of what it will cost probably will.

Even if the buyer is willing to accept the home in its

present condition, with its minor flaws, you can be certain of one thing—the buyer will expect you, the seller, to pay for these improvements indirectly by driving the purchase price of the home down.

All of these can be summarized in one sentence: Neat, clean, sharp homes sell, and quickly; shabby, dirty homes don't.

This indicates one thing: You should put your home into as good condition as you possibly can before you allow even one prospective buyer to cross your front door's threshold. This will take some time and effort on your part, and some money, but there is no question that it will pay big dividends for you in the long run.

In a tough real estate market, where sellers outnumber buyers, it is particularly important that your home be as sharp as possible, sharper than the other homes potential buyers will be comparing it to.

DETERMINING WHICH IMPROVEMENTS ARE NECESSARY

Begin by carefully and thoroughly examining every room of your home with a notebook in hand. Jot down every minor and major flaw and what it will take to repair it. Check the basement, the exterior, the roof, and the yard. Some of the things to check for are listed below:

1. Are the walls clean? Children's (and adult's) hands often smudge walls, and a little washing, or perhaps repainting, might be required.

2. Are there cracks in the walls? If so, patching plaster and painting may be required to make them look like new. You might also consider paneling a wall or two, but don't overdo it.

3. Are the colors of your walls universally appealing,

or will they appeal only to someone with unusual or unique tastes? You should disregard your personal likes and dislikes in color schemes at this point and keep in mind that it is *the buyer* you are attempting to appeal to. If you have doubts about proper colors, consult a home decorating center, paint store, or wallpaper shop for advice.

As inconsequential as it may seem, many a home sale has been lost because the wall paint or wallpaper was too unusual or different.

4. Are there cracks in the ceiling? If so, they should be patched and repainted.

5. Are there water stains on the ceiling (often caused by an overflowing bathtub, toilet, or leaky faucet)? If so, they *must* be repaired. Leaving the stains there and trying to explain to a prospective buyer that no problem exists is foolish. Either the buyer won't believe you or the buyer will dread the task ahead of having to repair the ceiling.

First, make certain that the problem that caused the water stain has been corrected. Simply painting or wallpapering over the stain usually will not cover it up—the stain will seep through your new cover. Therefore, you must first neutralize the stain. Check with a home decorating center, paint store, or wallpaper shop for a commercial product to use. If you cannot find such a product, try several coats of liquid shoe polish before painting or wallpapering.

6. Are any windowsills water stained? Although many buyers may not notice or may not be particularly alarmed if they do notice, it is a good precaution to sand and refinish. Make sure that the problem that caused the water stains has been remedied or your efforts will be for naught.

7. How's the woodwork? If it is scratched, chipped, or scarred, it should be refinished or touched up.

8. Are there any cracked windowpanes? If so, they should be replaced.

9. Are any doorknobs, cabinet knobs, and so forth inoperable or missing? A buyer may fear not being able to find a matching replacement. Therefore, you should replace or repair those items.

10. Are there any leaking faucets or water pipes? Buyers might consider these leaks to be a much bigger problem than they actually are. Call in a plumber if necessary.

11. Are the carpets clean? If not, shampoo them. It may be necessary to utilize a professional cleaning service to restore the carpet to like-new cleanliness.

12. Are the carpets worn? If so, you may need to replace them with new carpet to make the home attractive. Be careful to select a color and style that will be universally appealing. Do not install carpet that will appeal to only unusual or unique tastes.

Good quality, durable carpet does not necessarily have to be expensive. If you plan ahead sufficiently, you can probably make a good buy at one of the many carpet sales.

If new carpet is definitely warranted, but you prefer to let the buyer make his or her own selection, it is recommended that you offer the buyer a *carpet allowance*. That is, you should determine what an acceptable grade of carpet will cost and then pay that amount to the buyer on the day you close the sale. As you show the home, inform each prospective buyer that you are providing this carpet allowance.

13. Is all carpeting firmly attached to all floors and steps? If not, have a carpet layer stretch and tack the carpet so that it fits properly.

14. Are there any leaks in the roof? No buyer wants to inherit this problem, and it is definitely one that should be fixed.

15. Do any doors or windows stick or close improperly? Perhaps some rehanging, planing, or sanding will be required.

16. Do all built-in appliances like the garbage disposal, furnace, air conditioner, water heater, built-in fans, or other fixtures work properly, smoothly, and quietly? If not, have them repaired or replaced.

Usually, the sales contract calls for the seller to warrant that these items are in good working condition on the date of the closing of the sale. Therefore, if you don't repair or replace them now, you will probably end up having to do it eventually, anyway.

17. Are any light bulbs burned out? Are there any light switches or outlets that don't work?

Prospective buyers prefer to view the home when it is well lighted. If a light doesn't come on, the prospect will wonder whether it is a burned-out light bulb or if the switch or wiring is shot. Eliminate that concern by replacing any burned-out light bulbs and by having all light switches and outlets in proper working order.

18. Does your furnace look like it's about to gasp its last breath? If so, only the most daring and adventuresome of buyers will take the gamble that it will keep on working. Although this can be an expensive replacement, it may be *necessary* in order for you to sell your home.

Have the furnace checked by one or more reputable dealers. If they certify that the furnace is in good operating condition and should keep on working for a long time, solicit a written statement from them to that effect. You can show this to prospects to ease their minds. If, on the other hand, these dealers determine that the furnace needs to be replaced, you should do so.

The same consideration should also be given to your air-conditioning system and hot water heater.

19. Are there any annoying odors in the home from sewer pipes, pets, garbage cans, or other sources? This

will alienate a prospective buyer faster than almost any-thing. The source of the problem should be eliminated rather than attempting to cover up the odor with per-fumes or air fresheners.

If you have a house pet that smells, sheds hair, or soils the carpet and furnishings, relegate it to garage, an out-building, or a pet house outdoors. Even though you love that pet, it may cost you the sale if you keep it indoors.

20. Are clothes closets neat and uncluttered? Since it is impossible to determine the design of shelves and the amount of space from the outside of a closet, most pros-pects want to look inside. Neat closets help convey the message that there is sufficient storage space in the home for everything to be stored in its proper place. Messy closets indicate that there isn't enough room for everything.

21. Are all kitchen cabinets, bathroom cabinets, shelves, and storage areas clean and in order? Well-kept areas indicate roominess.

22. Do you have a "junk room" that is untidy? Neat-ness throughout the home will indicate that you have treated your home with care.

23. Are all stair steps free of objects? Are countertops attractive and free of needless clutter? Neatness here, too, will help portray the spaciousness of your home and the care you have given it.

24. Are your furniture and furnishings clean, neat, and uncluttered? Just like the saying "Clothes make the man," it can be said to some extent that "Furniture makes the home." The general appearance of the home, even the furniture and furnishings, add to the overall impression the prospective buyers will receive.

Arrange your furniture as attractively as you can to display the roominess and versatility of the home. Avoid having needless pieces of furniture sitting around that make the rooms appear small and cramped.

If you must leave your home before it is sold and have

the option of leaving your furniture in the home (until it is sold) or taking it with you when you leave, it is generally best to leave the furniture in the home. A furnished home helps give the buyer an idea of what the home will look like when he or she moves their furniture in. Also, the furniture often helps mask those traffic patterns in the carpet or the faded wall paint or wallpaper.

25. Do you have any unfinished remodeling projects? Prospective buyers often worry if that missing ceiling tile will be installed, if that trim board will be finished, or if the loose electrical wires will be hooked up. Eliminate those concerns from your prospect's mind—finish those remodeling projects *completely* before putting your home on the market.

26. Does your basement leak water? Are there abnormally large cracks in the basement walls and/or floor? Few things will stop a buyer in his tracks like one of these problems.

If there are severe problems, it's probably best to face the facts. One way or the other, you will pay. If you leave the problem uncorrected, it will most likely take an extraordinarily long time to find a buyer who's willing to inherit that problem. Even then, the buyer will use that problem (and probably justifiably so) as a reason to drive the purchase price down to a far lower amount than you had anticipated.

A better solution is to fix the leaky basement or cracks even though it may be costly. Shop around, get estimates, explore alternative methods of solving the problem.

Once the problem is solved, you will have a saleable property. If the problem remains unsolved, the home is not very saleable—at least not at a good price and not very quickly.

The age and style of your home will largely dictate the necessity of having a basement that is in perfect condition. In a newer home, or in those cases where the basement will be used for living space, it may have much more importance than in an older home where the basement is virtually not used at all. Base your decision on whether or not to make extreme basement repairs on your estimation of the type of condition most buyers will expect the basement in a home like yours to be in.

27. How does the exterior of the home look? The appearance of your home from the outside, called *street appearance*, is very important since this is the first impression the prospect will get. If the prospect is turned off here, you may never get him or her inside the front door for a look at the rest of the home.

Is the siding in good condition. Are screen doors and screen windows in good shape? Is paint peeling? Is the color attractive and generally appealing to most tastes? If you must answer any of these questions negatively, take steps to correct the situation.

Do not, however, go overboard by installing expensive new siding on a low-priced home. Chances are you will never get even a fraction of your cost back. For example, let's assume you have a $75,000 home. If you spend $15,000 for new siding, you will have increased your investment in the home by 20% ($15,000 ÷ $75,000) for new siding alone. Undoubtedly, the new siding will improve the appearance of the home considerably and will unquestionably make it more saleable, but most likely it *will not* make it a $90,000 home, which is what you will now need to break even.

You would probably be far better off to invest $5,000 in a less expensive siding job, which would essentially serve your purpose as well as the expensive $15,000 siding. Now, with only $5,000 invested in siding, your chances of recouping your investment, and maybe even more for your efforts, are very good.

Certainly, you should not reside the home unless it is

absolutely necessary. A fresh coat of paint may be warranted, or perhaps a little touch up here and there, carefully applied, will suffice.

28. How reasonable are your heating costs? Heating costs have become a major concern for buyers, especially in regions that have cold winters. If your heating costs are reasonable for a home of your size and style, you have nothing to worry about. On the other hand, if your heating costs are outrageously high, you may need to consider adding some insulation to the sidewalls and attic to lower the heating costs. This can be expensive, but you can cut down on the costs considerably by doing all or some of the work yourself.

Adding insulation, if your home really needs it, may help improve saleability and may also pay for itself by helping you obtain a better sales price.

29. Are shrubs and bushes healthy and well trimmed? Is the lawn free of weeds and is the grass mowed? Perhaps a minor point, but a well-groomed yard helps sell the home.

30. In general, is your home as clean, neat, and attractive as you can make it? If so, it will certainly help sell the home as quickly and profitably as possible.

31. Are there any cherished or keepsake items that you will *not* want to leave with the home? Sometimes a chandelier, door chime, attached mirror, attached cabinet, or other fixture that would ordinarily stay with the home has great sentimental value, or you might simply want to keep the item for your next home.

If that's the case, remove the item, and replace it if necessary, *before* you show the home to any prospective buyers. That way you will avoid any confusion or misunderstandings about the item, and you will eliminate the possibility that the buyer will try to wrest the item away from you by stating in the offer that the item is to stay with the home.

WEIGHING THE COST OF IMPROVEMENTS

The foregoing list is presented to serve as a guide. In all cases, you must make your own decision whether or not any particular improvement will be worth the cost and the effort. In some cases, no doubt, the improvements that you're now considering are things that should have been done long ago and are necessary to bring the home back to a reasonable state of repair.

Carefully consider the cost of each improvement before you begin. In many cases, the improvements you make will substantially improve the ability to sell your home quickly. Although these improvements will also probably increase the amount you'll be able to obtain for your home, they often will not increase the value of the home much beyond what the improvements cost.

For example: If you spend $500 to paint the entire interior of your home, how much will that add to the value of the home compared to if you had left it unpainted? We might like to think that the paint job will add thousands of dollars to the sales price. In reality, though, that's normally not the case. What it will do is make the home more *saleable*, and, no doubt, you will also recoup your $500 cost, and perhaps a little more. If you do the work yourself, instead of hiring it out, your chances of making a profit above the cost of the improvement are greatly increased.

Carefully select the quality and price of materials used in making the improvements. In general, they should be in line with the overall quality and value of your home. If your home is expensive, then high-quality materials that match the rest of the home should be used. If your home is of relatively low value, use good grade but less expensive materials.

In all cases, do not go overboard by pouring great

sums of money into needless improvements for which you won't be able to recoup your investment. Keep in mind always that your goal is to improve the saleability of your home—the *profitable* saleability of your home.

Financing the Cost of Improvements

If you have readily-available cash that you can spare, this is the easiest way to pay for the cost of improvements to your home.

If you don't have the cash available, it will be worthwhile for you to borrow on a short-term basis. If you explain to the lender that you'll be able to repay the loan when your home sells, you should have no difficulty in obtaining the loan. The ideal situation will be to borrow on a basis whereby you do not need to make monthly payments, but rather repay the entire amount with interest after you receive the proceeds from your sale.

Your full-service bank where you have your checking account and savings account will be a good source to check first. Also, consider credit unions, small loan companies, and savings and loan associations.

4

Identifying Which Items Stay With the Home

Ordinarily, the sale of real estate includes "real estate and all that is permanently attached to the real estate." This may sound simple and clear enough, but in application, there are many gray areas that can be questionable. Are the drapes and curtains included? How about the wall-to-wall carpeting that is *not* tacked down? Does that full-length mirror stay? How about the curtain rods, that swag lamp, or the window air conditioner? All of these questions and others must be answered before you place your home on the market.

DISTINGUISHING BETWEEN PERSONAL PROPERTY AND FIXTURES

In determining which items do or do not stay with the home, property is classified in two categories: *personal property* and *fixtures*. Those items that are moveable and not attached to the home or land are called personal property and do not stay with the property.

Items that were once personal property but have now become permanently attached to the home or land are known as fixtures and are thereafter classified as real estate—they stay with the property when it is sold. A furnace would be an example of a fixture. Before it's installed in the home, it's personal property; once it's installed, it's classified as a fixture and becomes part of the real estate.

The following are lists of items that are ordinarily classified as either real estate and fixtures, or as personal property when a home is sold.

Real Estate and Fixtures (Included in the sale of the home)

1. Land.
2. House.
3. Outbuildings set on a permanent foundation or intended to be included with the sale. This would include a storage shed that has been attached to a foundation.
4. The furnace and other heating equipment that has been permanently installed.
5. Central air-conditioning unit.
6. Window air-conditioning units that have been permanently installed.
7. Water softener.
8. Built-in appliances such as the garbage disposal, dishwasher, range, and oven.
9. Built-in cabinets.
10. Light fixtures and door chimes.
11. Mirrors permanently attached to doors and walls.
12. Attached TV antennas, CB antennas, and the like.
13. All plumbing fixtures.

14. Permanently attached bars, counters, and the like.
15. All curtain rods and drapery rods.
16. Wall-to-wall carpet that is glued down or tacked down.
17. Window shades, venetian blinds, storm windows, storm doors, shutters, window screens, and door screens.
18. Automatic garage door openers and their control devices.
19. Attached mail boxes.
20. Clothesline poles permanently installed.
21. Outdoor yard fireplaces permanently installed.
22. All trees, bushes, shrubs, and other outdoor plantings.
23. Any other objects that are permanently attached to the home or land and whose removal would damage the property.

Personal Property (Not included in the sale of the home)

1. All personal items including furniture, and appliances that are not built in.
2. Carpet that is not glued down or tacked down. This includes carpet that extends wall-to-wall but is not attached. To avoid confusion and potential controversies, make sure you point these items out to the buyer in advance of signing an agreement to sell the home. It's a good idea explicitly to exclude any such items in your written agreement with the buyer.
3. Lamps that are not permanently installed but are plugged into a wall outlet. This includes a swag lamp hung from a hook in the ceiling and plugged into an outlet. If this type of lamp were permanently wired, it would stay with the home.
4. Fireplace tools and cut firewood.

5. Curtains and drapes. Although these are personal property and therefore need not stay with the home, it is *customary* that curtains and drapes are often left with the home, anyway. This is particularly true of living room, dining room, kitchen, family room, and other common living area rooms. If bedroom curtains match bedspreads or have particular sentimental value, they are usually removed by the seller of the home.

   The reason that curtains and drapes are often left with the home is that they are designed to be used in that home, would probably be expensive for the new owner to replace, and probably would be of relatively little future use or value to the seller, anyway. Also, it makes a very good selling point to be able to assure the buyer that the curtains and drapes will remain with the home.

6. Mirrors attached to walls or doors in such a fashion that they are not permanently affixed and can be removed without damaging wall or door surfaces.

7. Unattached, free-standing bars, counters, wall dividers, and the like. Since a prospective buyer might mistake these as attached or included with the home, make sure you point out that they do not stay.

   Even though these items might legitimately be classified as personal property, many sellers prefer to leave them with the home, anyway. This is because they are an integral part of the decor of the home, were designed for use in that home, and would probably be of little future use or value to the seller. Also, leaving these items with the property often helps make the home more saleable.

8. Storage sheds and other outbuildings that are not set on a foundation and were intended to be moveable.

9. Any other objects that are not permanently attached to the home or land and whose removal will not damage the property.

Taking Steps to Avoid Confusion

The preceding lists provide a good guideline to what items do and do not *ordinarily* stay with the home when it is sold. No doubt, there are other objects that might raise questions. To avoid confusion and possible controversies when the time comes to close the sale, follow one of the two following procedures:

- Clearly state to prospective buyers when you show them your home which items do and do not stay. Verbally pointing out these items will only create more confusion since memories tend to be inaccurate over a period of time. Therefore, make certain that you present the prospective buyers with a *written* list.

  When the sales agreement is drawn between you and the buyer, make certain it clearly states which items do and do not stay with the home.
- Remove any object that you do not intend to leave with the home and store it away before you show your home to any prospective buyer.

PERSONAL PROPERTY YOU MAY WANT TO LEAVE WITH THE HOME

In addition to those items that ordinarily stay with the home, there may be other items that you will *want* to leave. This might be because these items match the design and decor of the home, such as the moveable counters, bars, wall dividers, curtains and drapes previously mentioned. It might also include personal property like that huge freezer or old piano in the basement that will be just too difficult to remove.

If the stove and refrigerator match the decor and design of the home perfectly, you might consider selling them with the home as well. In some cases, you might even want to sell pieces of furniture that are particularly well suited to the design and color scheme of the home. This might especially be the case if these items will not fit in well in the new home you are moving to.

Rather than insisting that the buyer take these additional items of personal property, you might make them *optional* at the buyer's election. Therefore, if the buyer has his or her own items, or doesn't find yours to be particularly suited to their taste, they will not be forced to take something that they don't need or want.

If you have items of personal property that you agree to sell to the buyer, it might be best to follow this procedure: Include those items in the purchase price that any buyer would no doubt want to have remain with the home. Assign a price to each additional item you would consider selling and offer the buyer the opportunity to purchase them separately.

Your goal in making additional items of personal property available to the buyer should be to increase the saleability of the home, not hinder it. Therefore, remain as flexible as you can in regard to these items. This is particularly true in a tough market, where your buyer may also be considering several other homes. Your willingness to compromise on items of personal property may be the "little difference" that seals the sale.

Mineral Rights and Air Rights

Ordinarily, the sale of real estate includes the subsurface, known as *mineral rights* and the space above land, known as *air rights*. In residential areas, the mineral rights and air rights ordinarily have no particular value and are therefore routinely included in the sale of the property. To attempt to reserve these rights and sell only the surface rights (the land and home) would, no doubt, alarm the buyer and interfere with the sale of your property. Therefore, if yours is a normal residential property, you should expect that you will transfer all air, surface, and mineral rights with the sale.

If you own substantial rural acreage in an oil-, gas-, or mineral-producing area, it may be common practice to retain the mineral rights and sell only the surface rights and air rights. If you own real estate in a city area bounded by high-rise buildings, the air rights may have great potential value and you may wish to retain them. If the mineral rights and/or air rights do have value, you will, of course, decrease the saleability of your property by retaining these rights rather than transferring them to the buyer.

INSTRUCTIONS, GUARANTEES, AND TOUCH-UP MATERIALS

Most likely you have instruction booklets and/or guarantees for many of the fixtures included in the sale of your home. These might be for the furnace, air conditioner, garbage disposal, built-in dishwasher, built-in range and oven, water softener, and any other appliances or fixtures that are to be left in the home.

Potential buyers may fear that they'll be unable to find replacement parts or enforce guarantees on these items. Therefore, it's a good idea to round up these instruction booklets and guarantees and have them available to reassure the buyer. You should, of course, leave them behind for the buyer when you vacate the home after it's sold.

If you have any paint, stain, wallpaper, carpet, or

other materials left over from the construction or refurbishing of your home, you should gather these materials together in a convenient place. The buyer will be pleased with your thoughtfulness and will be relieved that materials and supplies will be available for any touch-up, patching, or repairs. If you do not have any leftover materials, develop a list of stores and other suppliers where you purchased the materials.

Providing the instruction booklets, guarantees, and touch-up materials for the buyer may not be a major force in the sale of your home, but it's one of several "little things" you can do to make your home a more attractive, appealing, and worry-free buy than others to which the buyer compares it.

5

Appraising Your Home

It's now time to determine the asking price for your home. This is one of the most crucial steps in the entire sales process and one that must be approached with painstaking care.

If your home is priced too low, you will cheat yourself out of money that you deserve; and, strange as it may sound, you will chase away some potential buyers because they will fear that something *must* be wrong with your home if you have it priced that low.

If the home is priced too high, buyers will recognize that fact and will bypass it in favor of other homes that are more reasonably priced. Sure, buyers could make you an offer at a lower price, but many buyers are reluctant to offer drastically less than the asking price for fear of embarrassing you and themselves alike. Also, many buyers prejudge that the seller won't take a huge drop in price, so they don't make an offer at all.

Another problem with overpricing the home is that it most likely won't sell at that price and will consequently sit on the market for a long time. Then, in an effort to sell the home, you will need to drop the price, often far below what you could have originally sold it for if it had been more reasonably priced. This is because a home that has been on the market for a long time without selling becomes "stale" and can develop a bad reputation in the community: the "Nobody else wanted to buy the Jones house, so I'm not going to buy it either" attitude. Also, if the home has been on the market a long time, buyers presume that the seller is getting desperate to sell (and often they are accurate) and will drive a hard bargain.

What all of this indicates is that you must find the one "right" asking price for your home that is neither too low nor too high.

Determining Market Value

The goal in appraising your home should be to find its *market value.* Market value is the price your home should bring if it's placed on the market for a reasonable length of time and is given proper exposure and promotion. There are many factors that will influence the market value of your home, including the following:

1. The national economy. The condition of the national economy affects the sale of all homes. If the economy is strong and if people have confidence in the government, in business, and in the future, the general attitude toward buying homes will be positive. On the other hand, if there is much uncertainty and pessimism, people will be less willing to make a long-term commitment to the future by purchasing a home.

2. The local economy. The real estate market is basically local in nature. The status of the economy in your community and your area will probably have a greater affect than the condition of the national economy on the market value and saleability of your home.

If a progressive, optimistic attitude prevails, if employment is high, business and industry is thriving, and new industry and thus more people are moving into your area, the housing market is likely to be very strong. If, however, there is high unemployment, layoffs, plant closings, and a generally sluggish local economy, homes will be harder to sell.

3. Interest rates. Most people do not have enough money to pay cash for the purchase of a home. Therefore, they must borrow a substantial portion of the purchase price from a lending institution. As interest rates increase, fewer persons are willing to borrow money. Also, higher interest rates mean higher monthly loan payments for the borrower. Since most borrowers have a limit on how much they can pay for loan payments per month, this results in the buyer's needing to buy a less expensive home than they could if interest rates were lower.

If favorably low interest rates do prevail, more people will be willing to borrow money to buy homes and their money will go farther, meaning that they can buy more expensive homes.

4. Supply of homes available. The supply of homes available compared to the demand for homes in your community is a major determinent of the market value and saleability of your home. If there are many homes similar to yours on the market, buyers can be selective and are also in a better position to bargain on purchase price. If there are few homes like yours on the market, and if buyer demand is strong, your chances for a quick sale improve.

5. Desirability of your home. The style, size, location, and condition of your home is very important. If your home is generally appealing in all respects, it should be very marketable. On the other hand, if it is of unusual design, size, or style, it may be appealing to only a small number of potential buyers.

6. Terms and conditions of the sale. The terms and conditions under which you are able to sell your home can affect the ease with which you can sell it and can also affect the sales price. If you are willing and able to sell on a basis that makes it easy for the buyer to obtain possession of your home, you can greatly increase its saleability and often increase the amount a buyer is willing to pay. If you are in a position to sell on a contract for *deed*, *lease-purchase* basis, rent with *option to buy*, or can assist in any way with the buyer's financing, you may be able to greatly increase the attractiveness of your home to potential buyers.

APPRAISAL METHODS

There are several different techniques that you can use to determine the accurate asking price for your home. You may be able to use just one of these methods to get satisfactory results, but most likely you will want to use several to verify your conclusion.

Since appraisal of real estate is a *judgment* rather than a science that can be reduced to specific formulas, the results obtained from each appraisal method will most likely not be exactly the same. Therefore, you will need to correlate the results of each appraisal method you use to reach one final figure.

Appraising one's own home is a difficult task, even for real estate salespeople and professional appraisers. This is because it is sometimes hard to separate the owner's emotions from the facts. As you compare your home with others and as you compile information, strive to be as unbiased as possible. Give a good deal of consideration to the professional opinions rendered by those who do not have the emotional involvement in the home that you do.

Using Comparables

When professional appraisers, real estate salespeople, and loan company appraisers determine the appraised value of residential property, they do so primarily by the use of *comparables*. That is, they compare the home they are appraising to other similar properties that have *recently sold* and derive the value of the home based on the comparison.

For example: Assume you have a 1,500 square foot, three-bedroom, ranch-style home. If a three-bedroom, ranch-style home of similar age, size, location, and with similar features recently sold for $95,000, it can be derived that your home should also sell at or about that $95,000 range. This analysis assumes, of course, that $95,000 was a fair and reasonable selling price without any unusual or extenuating circumstances involved.

Usually, the homes used for comparison are not exactly alike, and additions or subtractions must be made for the differences. For instance, if your home is larger than another that recently sold, is in better condition, has a better location, or has more expensive cabinetry, value would be added to your home. If your home has no fireplace whereas the other home did, or if you have a single garage and the other home had a double garage, value would be deducted.

In appraising your home through the use of comparables, the key is to select homes that are very similar to yours so that a minimal number of adjustments will need to be made for the differences. Try to find as many properties similar to yours as you can for comparison purposes; a minimum of three is recommended.

How do you find out the price at which other properties in your community recently sold? Certainly *do not* rely upon word of mouth, rumor, or even the testimony of the buyer or seller. Quite often, these sources are very unreliable. You can find out exactly what the property sold for, however, by checking the record of sale at the county courthouse, usually upon request, at the *County Recorder*'s office. This information is a matter of public record and you are entitled to see it.

You can also get an idea of prices being asked for comparable properties by attending open houses and by keeping yourself informed of other homes available for sale in your community. Keep in mind, though, that these are homes that have *not* sold and that their eventual sales prices may be substantially different than the current asking price.

Using The County Assessor's Appraised Value

The *County Assessor* has the responsibility to appraise real estate for taxation purposes. Methods of evaluating property vary widely from state to state and even from county to county within a state. Then, too, the evaluation of property within any county is often inconsistent.

Since the County Assessor's job is to appraise real property for taxation purposes, that appraisal is often far different from an appraisal intended to determine market value. Even in those states where the Assessor's appraised value is supposed to be 100 percent of market value, it is often lower, and sometimes higher.

What this indicates is that you should not necessarily rely on the Assessor's appraised value as an accurate appraisal of the market value of your home. However, even though the assessed values of real estate may not indicate it, the County Assessor is often very knowledgeable about market values in the county. Therefore, rather than relying on the official assessed value of your home for tax purposes, you might rely somewhat on the County Assessor's personal opinion. It would not be out of line for you to inform the County Assessor that you are planning to sell your home and ask for an opinion of its market value.

It should be pointed out that some buyers check the County Assessor's appraised value of a home before making an offer on it. Since buyers ordinarily like to rely on the lowest figure anyone tells them for a home they are contemplating buying, some buyers may assume your home is worth no more than the Assessor's official appraised value, particularly if it's considerably lower than your asking price. Knowing that the Assessor's appraised value for tax purposes does not necessarily reflect market value should be very helpful to you when negotiating with this type of buyer.

Hiring an Appraiser

One way to arrive at an asking price for your home is to hire an appraiser who is in touch with real estate values in your community. You might contact a professional appraiser, a real estate salesperson, a Federal Housing Administration (FHA) appraiser, or you might even hire a lending institution appraiser who "moonlights" by doing private appraisals after normal business hours.

Since you're paying for the appraisal and will have no future business dealings with that appraiser, the appraiser will have nothing to gain personally by giving you an appraisal that's purposefully higher or lower than market value (as a real estate salesperson seeking a listing or a lender's appraiser contemplating a loan might). You should, therefore, get as accurate an appraisal as that person can render. It should still be kept in mind, however, that this appraisal is only an estimate of value based on the appraiser's judgment and is only as accurate as the appraiser's ability allows. Therefore, it's highly important to choose a competent appraiser.

It's also important that you do not in any way influence or prejudice the appraiser's judgment or intimidate the appraiser by telling or hinting to him or her in advance of the appraisal what figure you want to or expect to hear. This might influence the appraiser's judgment and you may get an inaccurate appraisal because of it.

After the appraiser has rendered an opinion of the market value of your property, you will, of course, want to discuss the estimate with the appraiser.

Using Replacement Cost

If yours is a newer home (perhaps built within the last 20 years), the cost of rebuilding that same home at the same location today can be used as a guide. If yours is an older home, calculating *replacement cost* is often futile since building techniques, styles, and designs have changed considerably through the years, and a buyer might make many changes if he or she were to build a similar home today.

Determining the replacement cost of your home is not as easy as it might sound. Many contractors and lumber dealers might talk of $40, $50, $60, or $70 per square foot as building costs today, but those figures can be very deceiving without additional checking. Some builders include the cost of the building site, the garage, the basement, concrete driveway, and landscaping in their square-foot figure; others include only some of them.

Also, the cost of building a home can vary widely with the quality that goes into it. Solid hardwood trim, custom-made kitchen cabinets, plush carpeting, a finished basement, extra bathrooms, fireplaces, and a prime building site are just some of the areas where thousands of dollars might be added to the cost. Also, the cost of building the second story of the home is lower than the main floor because you already have the land, the foundation, and the basement.

In order to calculate an accurate replacement cost of your home, you will need first to gather some background information. Determine the exact square footage by measuring the exterior of your home. Make note of the type and dimension of lumber used for sidewalls, rafters, joists, underlayment, and so forth. Also observe the type of siding, shingles, windows, and doors on the home. Evaluate the interior of your home, the trim, cabinets, carpet, and any special features. Also, make certain you measure the garage.

Now, armed with some rather detailed information about your home, you're in a position to approach a contractor or lumber dealer for an *estimate* of replacement cost. Since you're not actually contemplating the construction of such a home, you may need to pay the contractor or lumber dealer for their efforts since otherwise you would be wasting their time. The contractor who built your home may be able to give you a quick, accurate, and inexpensive appraisal of the home's replacement cost.

The current value of your building site can be calculated quite accurately by comparing it with other parcels of similar size and location that have recently sold in your community. Also calculate what it would cost to replace the cement work for driveways and sidewalks, trees, bushes, shrubs, lawn seeding or sodding, and other landscaping.

The cost of building a home exactly like yours, on your lot, with your landscaping at today's prices should be the total of all of the components listed above. It should be quickly pointed out that the only sure way you could ever determine the *exact* replacement cost of your home would be to actually go ahead and build it. When all of the work was done and the bills were paid, then you would know. Your estimate of replacement cost, based on the procedure described above, however, should be accurate enough for your appraisal purposes.

Part of the value of knowing what it would cost to replace your home at today's prices is this: It basically sets the *maximum* amount that you could ever expect to receive for your home, in theory anyway. This is because if you're asking more for your "used" home than it would cost a buyer to build a brand-new one just like it, we would assume that the buyer would build rather than buy. In practice, things don't always work that way, though. Since the buyer could never duplicate your location, may not have the time or desire to build, and may not be aware of the replacement cost, it's possible a buyer might pay as much for your home as a new one would cost. This might be particularly true if your home is only a few years old, has an extremely desireable location, or has some other very appealing attractions.

As a general rule, existing homes sell for less than their replacement cost, often considerably less. Therefore, in appraising your home to determine its market value, you should rely much more heavily on the value determined by using comparables and on the appraised value rendered by a professional appraiser.

If your asking price is considerably lower than its replacement cost at today's prices, you have at your disposal a powerful sales tool. You can point out to prospective buyers the results of your research in calculating your home's replacement cost and show them the bargain they're getting by purchasing your home.

Using Your Cost Plus Inflation

If you purchased your home recently, within the past few years, you may be able to determine a fairly-accurate market value by adding the inflation rate to the price you paid when you bought or built the home.

The difficult part of this appraisal process is accurately to determine the rate of inflation to apply. The nationwide inflation rates on consumer goods or on real estate as quoted in the newspapers is not necessarily applicable to real estate prices in your community. In recent years, home prices have soared as much as 20%, 30%, or more in a single year in some communities, while in others the inflation rate was 5% or less, and in still others, prices dropped. This is because the real estate market is very local in nature and is greatly affected by the economic conditions within each community.

By doing a little research in your community, you may be able to determine a rate of inflation on homes that will be suitable to use for this appraisal process. This information might be available from a local newspaper article, the County Assessor's office, County Auditor's office, or from a local real estate association.

Let's assume that you have been able to determine that in the past 3 years since you purchased your home for $80,000, the inflation rates have been 5%, 7%, and 10%. To determine the value of your home through this process, apply each year's rate of inflation to the preceding year's value (see the table on page 48).

According to this appraisal basis, therefore, the value of the home after 3 years would be approximately $98,868. If you made significant improvements to your home that are beyond normal maintenance, the cost of these should be added to the results obtained above. Finishing off the attic or basement or building a new garage would be examples.

This appraisal procedure may not provide a precisely-accurate asking price, but it can be used as a rule of thumb to determine if your asking price seems to be reasonable.

Of course, if real estate values in your community have dropped in recent years, the cost-plus-inflation method will be ineffective in estimating your home's value.

COST PLUS INFLATION APPRAISAL METHOD

First Year:	$80,000	Purchase price
	× 5%	First year's rate of inflation
	$ 4,000	Increase in value for first year
	$80,000	Purchase price
	4,000	Increase in value for first year
	$84,000	Value at end of first year
Second Year:	$84,000	Value at beginning of second year
	× 7%	Second year's rate of inflation
	$ 5,880	Increase in value for second year
	$84,000	Value at beginning of second year
	5,880	Increase in value for second year
	$89,880	Value at end of second year
Third Year:	$89,880	Value at beginning of third year
	× 10%	Third year's rate of inflation
	$ 8,988	Increase in value for third year
	$89,880	Value at beginning of third year
	8,988	Increase in value for third year
	$98,868	Value at end of third year (Estimated)

Using the Opinions of Friends, Neighbors, and Relatives

The advisability of using the opinions of your friends, neighbors, and relatives in appraising your home can be summed up in one word—*Don't.*

Unless any of these people are real estate professionals, their judgment of your home's value will be only personal opinions—personal opinions packed with emotions, good intentions, wishful thinking, and/or jealousies. You should, therefore, generally disregard any opinions of your home's value these people give and make your own decision based on the facts you have been able to gather.

DETERMINING THE ASKING PRICE

Each home has its own market value and no amount of wishful thinking can change that. Your goal in appraising your home should be to determine that market value, whatever it might be.

Once you have determined as accurately as you can what price your home should bring, you must now decide on an *asking price*. Assume, for example, that you have determined that your home should be saleable for $95,000. What amount should you ask for the home when you actually put it on the market—$95,000, $97,000, $100,000, $115,000, or some other amount?

Before answering that question, two comments are in order: (1) You can always come down from your asking price, but you can never (usually, anyway) go up, and (2) If you are unsuccessful in trying to sell your home yourself, will you eventually list it with a real estate company? If so, and in accordance with the first comment, your asking price must *not* be lower than the price you will ask if you list with a real estate company.

There is a certain amount of difference of opinion about whether a home should be listed at its appraised market value, slightly above it, or greatly above it. Those (mostly the homeowners) favoring an asking price greatly above a home's appraised market value do so with the hope of snaring an unsuspecting buyer who will pay far more than the home is actually worth. Usually, buyers shop around before making a final selection and they are therefore quite knowledgeable about real estate property values. Consequently, only in rare situations will a buyer pay a price that is far greater than the actual value of a property.

Those favoring an asking price that is only slightly above the appraised market value do so to compensate for a possible error in appraising the home too low and to allow a little leeway for negotiating room.

Those favoring an asking price that is at the appraised market value do so because they believe one should ask only what the property is worth and no more.

It is recommended that you set an asking price that is right at or slightly above the appraised market value. This is particularly true in a tough real estate market, since grossly overpricing your home may chase buyers away and to homes that are more reasonably priced. For instance, if the appraised market value of your home is $95,000, an asking price in the $95,000–$98,500 range would be appropriate. Even at the $98,500 amount, you should not be so far overpriced that you will scare buyers away. Keep in mind that as owner of the home you are always in control of accepting or rejecting any offers that are presented to you. So, if an offer is submitted that is lower than you can accept, you can reject it or submit a counteroffer.

Select *one* amount as your asking price. If you tell a prospect that you are asking "$97,000 or $98,000," the buyer will automatically think in terms of the lowest amount you state. You should state a firm "$97,000" or a firm "$98,000," but not both amounts.

6

Identifying Your Home's Best Selling Points

Every home has its own special appeals. What's yours?
To answer that question, you might think back to the
reasons you had when you bought the home. Chances
are, those same factors will also appeal to your prospective buyers. Some strong selling points are listed below:

1. Location. Real estate experts almost universally
agree that location is the single most important factor
when buying a home. Therefore, you should first analyze
the advantages that your location has to offer. Regardless of where your home is located in the community,
there are probably several good reasons why that location is appealing, including some of the following:

a. Convenience to shopping areas.
b. Quiet, peaceful area.
c. Easy access to highways and/or public transporta-
tion systems.

    d. Established neighborhood with proven property
      values.
    e. Friendly, helpful neighbors.
    f. Nearness to playgrounds, parks, swimming pool,
      tennis courts, and other recreational facilities.
    g. Nearness to schools, churches, and hospitals.
    h. Many children for playmates.
    i. Exclusive and/or prestigious area.

2. Street appearance. Walk out on the street in front of your home and take a look. Is your home attractive? If you were a prospective buyer, would you want to look inside? These are exactly the questions your prospects will be asking themselves. An attractive-looking home set on a well-manicured lot will lure buyers to want to learn more about your home.

3. First impression. Remember the first time you ever set foot inside your home? What was it that appealed to you or struck you?

This is the same type of impression your prospects will receive. Since first impressions are so strong and long-lasting, a substantial part of a buyer's decision to buy or not to buy your home will be made at that instant. A thought will flash through the prospect's mind—either "I like this home," or "I don't like this home." If that first impression is positive, you're off to a good start; if it's negative, you'll have an extremely difficult time ever convincing this prospect to buy.

Every home has a character of its own. What's yours? Is it warm, homey, elegant, spacious, cozy, charming, or roomy? Even though this is an intangible, it is real and may be one of your home's most important selling points. You might point out to your prospects the type of feeling you think your home possesses.

4. Lot size. Many people place great importance on the size of the lot on which the home rests. Families with children might like a big yard for play space. A fenced-in

yard is an extra bonus. A small yard might be very appealing to elderly buyers or to those who are away from home a lot since there won't be much lawn to mow.

Prospective buyers who have a pet dog may be as concerned about their pet's welfare as they are of their own. Therefore, a yard suitable for a dog house or dog run might be a great attraction.

5. Number of bedrooms. The number of bedrooms a home has is one of the main distinguishing features used to describe a home. If a married couple has two children—a boy and a girl—a two-bedroom home just won't do. They will want at least a three-bedroom home. An elderly couple with no children at home might find a home with more than two bedrooms to be unnecessary.

Regardless of the number of bedrooms your home has, it will be appealing to some size family. Identify as closely as you can the various sizes of family that could comfortably fit into your home.

6. Kitchen size. The size and arrangement of the kitchen is ordinarily one of the major concerns of a buyer. If yours is a large kitchen, you can point out the spacious eating area, plentiful cupboards and storage space, and expansive food preparation area.

If your kitchen is small, you can point out the efficient arrangement and handy step-saving design.

7. Storage space. If your home has an abundance of storage space, you have a good selling point here. This is one of the things your home probably cannot have too much of, so point out every possible storage area.

8. Interior arrangement. The arrangement and usage of the interior of your home can offer several attractions. If your home has some of the following, they should be emphasized:

a. At least two bedrooms on the same floor. This is a must in the eyes of most parents with a small child.

 b. A bathroom on the main floor. This saves a lot of running up and down stairs.

 c. At least one bedroom on the main floor. This can be a great asset, even a necessity, for elderly buyers.

 d. Main-floor laundry room. This is a great step-saving attraction.

 e. Good separation of frequently used rooms for noise control.

 f. Privacy of bedroom, den, or office area.

 g. Easy access to the basement from outdoors.

 h. Stairways that allow easy movement of furniture.

 i. Mud room or other entryway where soiled clothing, shoes, and boots can be removed and stored.

 j. Rooms of extraordinary size, particularly a bedroom, kitchen, or recreation room.

9. Ease of care and maintenance. No one wants to be a slave to their home. Buyers will appreciate any of the following time- and money-saving features.

 a. Permanent siding that does not require painting or that has a guarantee.

 b. Vinyl or linoleum floor coverings that do not require waxing.

 c. High-quality carpet that will wear for years.

 d. Wall coverings that can be wiped off rather than repainted when smudges appear.

 e. Storm windows or combination windows whose exterior can be cleaned from the inside of the home.

 f. A home in overall well-maintained condition, with no repairs or improvements necessary.

10. Efficiency. In these times of uncertain energy costs, one of a buyer's first concerns is the cost of utilities. If your home has low heating and cooling costs, that should be emphasized as a strong selling point. Some of the following will favorably impress your prospects.

a. Adequate insulation in sidewalls and attic.
b. Efficient, energy-saving furnace, air conditioner, and water heater.
c. Low voltage built-in appliances.
d. Auxiliary heating from woodburning furnace, solar unit, or other source.
e. Thermal windows that afford extra energy savings.
f. Superior weather stripping around doors, caulking around windows, and so forth that make the home tighter.
g. Thermal drapes and curtains that aid in heating and cooling.
h. Shelter from the elements by trees and other wind-breaks.

11. Quality. Most buyers are impressed with high quality. Some of the things in your home that you take for granted might fall within this category, including the following:

a. High-quality construction including building tech-niques, and grade, type, and dimension of lumber used.
b. Natural wood doors, trim, and cabinets.
c. High-quality, name-brand built-in appliances, fur-nace, windows, doors, siding, carpet, and so forth.
d. Quality cabinets, door handles, cabinet fixtures, etc.
e. Extraordinary features like built-in cabinets, shelves, cedar closet, and so forth.

12. Special features. Often it is the special features that set one home apart from another. Often, too, a buyer has a certain special feature in mind that's of overriding im-portance. Not all of the special features listed below will be looked upon with equal importance by all prospects,

but to the right buyer, one of these features may sell the home almost by itself.

a. Large garage suitable for two or three cars and/or a workshop.
b. Large game room area suitable for a pool table, Ping-Pong table, or similar usage.
c. Walk-in closets.
d. Home office area or sewing room.
e. Workshop area.
f. Large deck or patio.
g. Special interior or exterior lighting.
h. Ideal yard for a prized family pet.
i. Storage shed for lawn and garden tools.
j. Bedroom large enough for a huge bedroom set.
k. Electric garage door opener.
l. Two, three, or more bathrooms.
m. Swimming pool, tennis court, hot tub, greenhouse, etc.
n. One or more fireplaces.
o. Bar or lounge area.
p. Formal dining room.
q. Cedar closet.
r. Main-floor laundry room.
s. Any special-purpose room like a dark room.
t. "Gadgets" that make living more comfortable and enjoyable, like a computerized thermostat.
u. Handicap-accessible home with entry ramp and wide hallways and stairs.
v. Extremely low real estate taxes.

13. Special terms. Attractive terms and arrangements, like those listed below, can set your home apart from others on the market and make it easy for the prospect to buy.

a. Special financing arrangements that will make it easy for the prospect to buy with little or no down payment or that will make it easy to obtain a real estate loan.

b. Allowing a possession date that will fit exactly into the buyer's time schedule.

CAPITALIZING ON YOUR STRONGEST SELLING POINTS

If your home possesses some of these strong selling points, emphasize them in your promotion and advertising and call them to your prospect's attention as you show them your home. You can't always expect that your prospects will recognize these advantages by themselves; you must point them out and emphasize the advantages that your special features will provide.

7

Promoting the Sale of Your Home

Promoting the sale of your home should consist of more than just writing an ad, placing it in your local newspaper, and sitting back and forgetting about it. You must get out and *sell* your home.

Your goal should be to contact every potential prospect and to get them inside your home. The more people you contact, the better your chances of making a quick sale—and a profitable one.

PROMOTIONAL TECHNIQUES

No one medium or promotional method will reach all potential buyers. You'll have best results if you combine several different techniques into a promotional program. No single technique listed below may produce dazzling results by itself, but a combination of several of them in a coordinated program should bring a truly amazing response.

Plan your promotional program in advance. Coordinate all the activities so that they impact at the same time or in some logical sequence.

Some of the following promotional techniques will cost only some of your time. Others will also cost money, but that cost will be relatively insignificant compared to what you'll save by selling your home yourself. Don't try to cut corners or pinch pennies here. Spend whatever is necessary, without going overboard, to make every potential prospect aware that your home is for sale.

1. Tell your neighbors. Maybe one of them will want to move down the street to your home. They have already shown that they approve of the neighborhood—after all, they live there. If none of your neighbors has an interest, perhaps they will have a friend or relative they would like to have nearby.

Go door to door, informing every neighbor within a two- to three-block radius. Ask them if they have an interest in your home or know of someone else who might. Hand them an information sheet (see page 118) on your home.

2. Think back. Has anyone who visited your home expressed admiration for it or stated that some day they would like to have a home like yours? If so, you have an excellent prospect.

3. Sit down and make a list of people who you think might be a prospect for your home. This might include friends, neighbors, relatives, work associates, and any other names you can come up with, even if you don't know the people on a personal basis. Don't leave any names out and don't prejudge whether someone may or may not be interested in your home—let them make that decision for themselves.

4. When you come in contact with people at work or at social gatherings, tell them that you're selling your home. Ask them if they have an interest and to pass the word along to anyone they know who might be interested in buying a home.

5. Post notices on community service bulletin boards or bulletin boards at work. Follow acceptable ad-writing procedures in preparing your notice.

6. Place advertisements in local newspapers and advertising supplements. Consider placing an advertisement on your local radio station.

If there's an influx of people moving to your area from another community because of plant closings, transfers, or whatever, consider advertising your home in the local media in that community.

7. Place advertisements in organizational newsletters published by the Elks, Kiwanis, or other similar groups, if possible.

8. Give particular attention to people who are currently renting. Many of them will, no doubt, purchase a home some day and your contacting them may be the stimulus they need.

You may be able to gather names of renters by searching the telephone directory for addresses of people living at known apartment complexes. If you're in an apartment building, you might jot down names from mailboxes or door tags and later telephone these people.

9. Your local newspaper is a good source of potential buyers that you can contact. The recently engaged, newly married, or new parents have all had a significant change in their life-styles. Many of them will soon purchase their first home or will need a larger one.

People who have just received a job promotion (and most likely a hefty pay raise, too) are also often featured in the local newspaper and are worth contacting.

10. Contact major employers (the personnel director,

the owner, or the manager) in your community. Tell them that you're selling your home and ask them to mention it to new employees moving in from out of town. You might even drop off copies of an information sheet for them to pass along.

This can be an excellent technique since if an employer recommends to a new employee that they consider looking at your home, the employee will probably do it.

11. Place a For Sale sign in your front yard where passersby will notice it. Make the sign large and attractive and place it where it can be easily seen.

You may want to hold off doing this for a few weeks until you have had a chance to run some of your advertisements and make some personal contacts of your own. If your For Sale sign is displayed too long, your home may develop a reputation of being "stale."

12. As you talk to each person about your home, *ask* if they know of anyone who might be a good prospect for you to contact. Most people will gladly volunteer names if they know of someone. This is a prospecting technique that's widely and successfully used by life insurance salespersons and real estate agents to develop an endless chain of potential clients.

13. Consider holding an open house. Advertise it widely in advance. Hold it at a time that will be attractive to most people—weekend afternoons are ordinarily ideal.

Since you may have dozens or even hundreds of lookers, you may need some assistance in conducting your open house. Recruit several friends to help you.

Have each guest sign their name, address, and telephone number in a guest register. Talk to as many guests as you can personally. Ask them questions early on in your conversation to determine if they are merely sightseers or if they are potential buyers.

Since you may not be able to spend as much time as you would like describing all aspects of your home to each prospect, you will find it ideal to have duplicated information sheets about your home that can be distributed.

You may or may not want to serve refreshments. If you do, keep them simple, inexpensive, and of the variety that won't soil the carpeting if dropped or spilled.

Within 3 or 4 days following your open house, contact persons who attended to see if they do have any interest in your home. This can be easily done via the telephone.

You will probably find it best to try your other promotional and prospecting techniques before holding an open house. This is because it's often easy to overlook a solid prospect in the bedlam atmosphere that prevails with many people milling around during an open house. You will be better off if you can locate those same prospects individually and show them your home on a one-to-one basis.

BE AGGRESSIVE

Actively and aggressively pursue the sale of your home. Do not expect prospects to volunteer to knock on your door—go out and find them. Follow up on every lead *immediately*, no matter how improbable it might seem. Certainly, you will go on a lot of wild-goose chases and will wind up at a lot of dead ends; this is to be expected, but somewhere there is someone who will want to buy your home, and your job is to follow up on every lead until you find that *one* buyer.

When you get the name of a prospect from one of your promotional activities, call them on the telephone, invite them to your home, or go to see them in person.

MAKING TELEPHONE CALLS

When you place a telephone call, you have a distinct advantage over the person you are calling. You are selecting the topic of conversation and you can prepare yourself in advance. Organize some notes that you can use for reference, or develop a script that you can read to get started. Once you've made your opening statement, the conversation will develop into normal, two-way communication. You can use the following scripts as a guide, but you may need to develop your own to fit your own situation.

Cold Call to Someone You Do Not Know

"Hello, this is (*your name*). I live at (*your address*) and I'm selling my home by myself, without the aid of a real estate company. (*Prospect's name*), someone told me that you are thinking of buying a home and I'm calling to invite you to come look at my home. Will it be possible for you to stop over to look at it tonight?"

Call to a Newly Engaged

"Hello, this is (*your name*). I read in the (*name of your newspaper*) that you recently became engaged and will be getting married soon—Congratulations! (*Prospect's name*), I'm selling my home and the thought occurred to me that since you'll be soon getting married, you may be in the market for a home. Are you and (*name of prospect's future spouse*) thinking of buying a home?"

Cold Call to Someone Who Is Presently Renting

"Hello, (*prospect's name*), this is (*your name*). I understand that you're currently renting, is that correct?

(Prospect will reply) (*Prospect's name*), I'm selling my home and I know that many people who rent would prefer to invest in their own home instead of collecting rent receipts. (*Prospect's name*), I'd like to invite you to come look at my home, and if you like it, perhaps we can work out an arrangement for you to buy it."

Follow-Up Calls

After someone has looked at the home but has not given you a definite yes or definite no, follow up to check their interest.

Make your first follow-up call one, two, or three days after the prospect looked at the home. On this call, don't be overly aggressive or pushy. It's ideal if you can call to deliver some additional information they requested or to relay something important you "forgot" to tell them.

First Follow-Up Call

"Hello, (*prospect's name*), this is (*your name*). I (or my spouse and I) enjoyed having you look at my (our) home earlier this week. You asked if it would be possible to cement in a part of the backyard for a basketball court without getting a city building permit. I checked with the City Planning Office for you and they said a permit would be required, but that most likely it would be granted and that the cost would be only ten dollars. Did you have any other questions or concerns about the home?

"I know it's often difficult to remember everything after looking at a home just once. Would you like to come back to take a second look?" (Note: Try to set up a definite appointment.)

Second (or third) Follow-Up Call

"Hello, (*prospect's name*), this is (*your name*). It has been about a week since I talked to you, and I'm calling to check on what interest you might have in my home."

Follow-Up Call If You Lower Asking Price

If you drop the price of your home, make a follow-up call to every prospect on your list. Perhaps your new price will rekindle their interest.

"Hello, (*prospect's name*), this is (*your name*). It has been some time since I talked with you about my home. I (or we) have decided that perhaps the asking price was a little high and I (or we) have lowered the price by $1,500 to (state your new price). Do you think you would have an interest in the home at this new price?"

BE PERSEVERING

Do not give up on a prospect easily. If someone expresses an interest in your home, keep in touch with them. Here you must walk a fine line between keeping in touch, on the one hand, and being seemingly over anxious, high pressure, or overbearing, on the other.

Keep written records of all prospects and your contact with them. Write down anything a prospect says that might be of value to you in your future contact with them. A card file might be ideal for this purpose.

Don't expect to necessarily sell your home on the first day or during the first week. Don't get discouraged. Stick with it and actively work at selling your home through the weeks or perhaps even months that it will require to locate that one prospect who likes your home well enough to step forth and buy it.

8

Writing Your Advertisement

The purpose of your advertisement is to arouse the prospects' curiosity and to stimulate interest enough so they'll want to find out more about your home. This goal is the same whether your advertisement will be in a newspaper or advertising supplement, on the radio, or in the form of a poster displayed on some bulletin board, or whether the market is "strong" or "soft."

PREPARING THE COPY

Follow the principles listed below in preparing your advertising copy:

    1. Make the ad enticing and inviting. Make your home sound like it's too good to pass by without checking out.

    2. Use a caption or heading that will grab the reader's attention.

3. Do not list all of your home's features. Tell only enough to stimulate the prospects' interest to find out more. You're probably better off by telling too little than by telling too much. If you tell too much, many prospects will prejudge that your home is not suitable and will never contact you to find out more.

4. Select words and phrases, like those shown below, that describe your home in glowing terms that will stimulate your prospects' interest.

These terms might be used as a caption or heading at the top of your ad, within the body of the ad, or at the end of the ad as a final tag.

a. General Promotional Terms
1. First time available.
2. Priced below market value.
3. Owner must sell.
4. Priced below replacement cost.
5. Must sell—leaving town.
6. For sale by owner.
7. Shown by appointment only.
8. Priced for quick sale.
9. Best buy in town.
10. This one won't last long.
11. Priced below appraised value.
12. For sale by original owner.
13. Call today.
14. Move right in.
15. June 1 possession (or some other appropriate date).

b. Describing Your Location
1. Quiet area.
2. Cheerful neighborhood.
3. Wonderful neighbors.
4. Near schools.
5. Within walking distance to . . .

    6. Handy location.

    7. Picturesque view.

    8. Wooded area.

    9. Private setting.

  10. Easy access to shopping.

  11. Great neighborhood for children.

  12. Exclusive neighborhood.

  13. Gorgeous view.

  14. Peaceful location.

  15. Northeast location (or whatever your general location is).

c. Describing Your Home's General Condition

    1. Sparkling throughout.

    2. Immaculate condition.

    3. Well-kept.

    4. First-rate condition.

    5. Well cared for.

    6. Quality throughout.

    7. Spotless.

    8. In flawless condition.

    9. Newly painted (or carpeted, or shingled, etc.).

  10. Sharp!

  11. Gracious living.

  12. Energy efficient.

  13. Low heating costs.

  14. Many extras.

  15. Elegant.

d. Describing Your Home's Features

    1. Spacious kitchen.

    2. Handy kitchen.

    3. Huge master bedroom.

    4. Walk-in closets.

    5. Winding staircase.

    6. Custom-made cabinets.

    7. Cozy family room.

    8. Formal dining room.

    9. Charming throughout.

10. Efficient design.
11. Step-saving design.
12. Roomy double garage.
13. Care-free siding—never paint again.
14. Abundant storage space.
15. Large bathroom.

5. Write each advertisement carefully. Spend some time on it and rework it until it looks and sounds appealing.

6. Be honest. Even though a good real estate ad should be leading, it should not be misleading. Don't try to trick people into looking at your home by saying things that aren't true.

7. Your home will not appeal to everyone. It will be too large for some, too small for others. The price range will be too high for some, not high enough for others, and so on.

Identify what characteristics an ideal potential buyer is likely to possess, and gear your advertising and promotion toward that type of buyer. If your home will most likely appeal to a prospect with a certain family size, income, or special interest, highlight those factors in your advertising as illustrated below:

a. If yours is a small, one- or two-bedroom home, it will most likely be appropriate for a single person, the newly married, or the elderly.

b. If yours is a huge home, it will be more appealing to a family than to a single person or the elderly.

c. If your home is a modest, low-priced home in an average neighborhood, it will be most suitable for the working class rather than the upper class.

d. If yours is a high-priced home, you will need to appeal to the wealthy.

8. Develop your full advertising campaign in advance. Establish a series of ads that will run in a logical sequence. Change your ads periodically, perhaps each

week. If a particular advertisement brings greater response than others, use it more often.

ADVERTISING IN A TOUGH MARKET

In a slow real estate market, the tendency might be to write advertisements that are filled with urgency and desperation. Rather than paint a picture of a seller—you—who is so desperate that they will virtually give their property away, emphasize the positive selling points of your home.

Remember, if you are trying to sell your home in a tough market, all other home sellers are likewise operating in that same tough market. Emphasize that your home is neat, clean, sharp, and priced at market value for today's market. This is all a buyer can expect, and it is more than they will get from many sellers.

EXAMPLES OF ADVERTISEMENTS

Each of the advertisements shown below describe the same three-bedroom, ranch-style home with an asking price of $97,500. Perhaps you can use some of them as a guide in preparing your own advertisements.

Some of the ads are in straight-forward business language; others take a more rambling or humorous approach.

Remember that your goal is to attract attention and stimulate interest. Which of the following are the most appealing to you?

FIRST TIME AVAILABLE

Sparkling 3-BR ranch in a quiet northeast location. Huge master bedroom, spacious kitchen. Priced below market value.

362–5740

YOU'LL LOVE

the peaceful serenity of living in Danburry Heights. Newer home. Large rooms. Double garage. Priced to sell. For sale by original owner.

Call 362–5740

MY WIFE CRIED

when I told her we were moving. She doesn't want to leave her dream house—but we must. She'll miss the spacious kitchen, the cozy family room and the electric garage door opener. I'll miss the huge master bedroom and my handy workshop. The kids will miss the short walk to school and their great friends in the neighborhood. Our pride—your joy—come take a look.

362–5740

A RANCH

style home in a quiet northeast location. Quality construction. Spotless condition. Priced to sell.

362–5740

WE'LL SPLIT

the commission with you. Lovely ranch home in great neighborhood. Many fine features. Priced below appraised value. Worth a look. 362–5740

For Sale by Owner

FOR SALE BY OWNER

Leaving town—must sell

- 3 Bedrooms
- Roomy Kitchen
- Energy Efficient
- Near Schools
- Great Neighborhood

CALL 362–5740
for appointment to see

BEST BUY

in town. That's easy to say—but in this case, it's true! Immaculately clean, near-new 3-BR ranch. Priced in the $90's. Before you buy, check this one out.

362–5740

MOTHER-IN-LAW

said I was stupid for selling my home this cheap. For once she's probably right—but I'm in a hurry to move, a real hurry. Come look at my 3-bedroom ranch with huge master bedroom, spacious kitchen, double garage, and lots of other dandy features. I'll even throw mother-in-law in on the deal at no extra charge.

362–5740

DRIVE BY

1606 Danburry Heights. Beautiful oak woodwork, quality construction, large rooms. Priced lower than you'd think.

Call 362–5740
or
Stop in Anytime.
FOR SALE BY OWNER

(Note: You might leave this type of ad, with your address shown, until after some of the other ads have run.)

OPEN HOUSE

1606 Danburry Heights

Saturday, June 6:
1:00 PM–5:00 PM

Sunday, June 7:
1:00 PM–5:00 PM

Stop in—Take a look
Everyone welcome
For Sale by owner

OPEN HOUSE

9

Understanding the Buyer

No one has ever been able to pinpoint exactly why a buyer purchases what he or she does. In many cases, even the buyer would be hard pressed to explain their motives. Even though this is the case, most home buyers are usually motivated by certain common considerations.

1. Perceived needs. All home buyers are looking for a home that fits their needs as they see them. These needs may be in terms of size requirements (often measured in the number of bedrooms), prestige, location, or a dozen other factors.

2. Price range. Almost every buyer has a limit on the amount of money they can spend on a home. Their goal is to get as much home as they can for their money.

Even though prospective buyers may *think* they should be buying in a certain price range, their financial ability may restrict them to a less expensive home, or allow them to spend more than they anticipated.

3. Self-image. Whether they are consciously aware of it or not, buyers attempt to buy a home that fits in with

and enhances their self-image. If someone views himself as being conservative, he will buy a conservative, basic home rather than an extravagant one. If someone views himself as being modern, sophisticated, rich, creative, or whatever, he will seek a home that matches that image.

You can probably get a good idea of the type of prospect you are dealing with by observing their dress, automobile, speech, jewelry, grooming, and mannerisms.

4. Good Value. A constant fear of home buyers is that they are paying too much for the home and are not getting a good value. In a tough market, the buyer may be seeking a *particularly good value* or a "steal." You may need to convince the buyer, regardless of market conditions, that your home is priced at market value for today's market and is worth the money because of the many benefits in quality, size, location, and other features they are receiving.

5. Unlimited wants. Most buyers have a mental image of the ideal "dream house" they would like to have. Often, that dream house, with the sunken living room, fireplaces, huge bedrooms, wooded lot, winding drive, and bubbling brook in the backyard doesn't exist, or if it did, they couldn't afford it. Therefore, it is sometimes necessary to try to help align the buyers' wants with reality.

6. Uncertainty. Many buyers *think* they know the size, style, and location of home they are looking for, but, in reality, they do not. Experienced real estate salespeople can tell you dozens of stories about prospects who insisted on buying a one-story, ranch-style home but ended up buying an older, two-story home instead. Or, the prospect who demanded two fireplaces but bought a home without any. Or, the buyer who required a double attached garage but bought a home with a single unattached garage. The stories could go on, but you get the idea.

Does all this mean that no buyer knows what he or she wants? No—many buyers have definite requirements and stick to them. Many other buyers, however, find that any number of styles and sizes of homes are suitable. Therefore, if a prospect states that he or she is looking for a home of a certain style or size that differs from yours, don't give up on them—they may really be looking for a home like yours but don't know it yet!

7. Apprehension. Buying a home is a big step, particularly for the first-time buyer. You may need to assure the prospect that this is a wise decision and a good investment. Using case histories of other people you have known who have purchased homes and then later sold them at a profit might be helpful.

8. Peer influence. All people are somewhat influenced by the expectations and attitudes of their friends, relatives, and coworkers. Therefore, prospective buyers will be influenced by their anticipation of what other people will think or say when they buy this home.

In some cases, you may need to convince prospective buyers that they need satisfy only themselves. In other cases, you may be able to appeal to the sense of pride the buyer will derive from showing this home to friends and relatives.

9. Predispositions. Many prospective buyers will have preconceived ideas about many factors pertaining to home buying. They may believe that a certain type of construction is good, another is bad. They may think one style of home is far superior to another, and so on. Many of these preconceived ideas may be factually correct, others may not be, and still others may be simply a matter of personal opinion.

If these predispositions favor your home, you can reinforce those ideas. If they are unfavorable, you may need to re-educate the prospect.

UTILIZING YOUR KNOWLEDGE OF BUYERS' MOTIVES

Try to develop as complete an understanding as you can of each prospect's needs, wants, and buying motives. You can then appeal to these by pointing out how your home will help satisfy their requirements.

10

Qualifying the Buyer

Often, buyers misinterpret their financial capabilities. Some shoot too high, others too low. You can help your own cause and help the buyer by being able to determine whether your asking price is within the prospect's financial ability. Making this determination will help you avoid pinning your hopes on making a sale to someone who obviously cannot afford your property.

DETERMINING THE BUYER'S FINANCIAL CAPABILITY

A buyer's financial capability is based upon three major factors: (1) the buyer's net worth, (2) the buyer's income, and (3) the buyer's character.

Net Worth

Net Worth is the difference between the prospect's assets and liabilities—that is, the difference between all that is owned and all that is owed. This is ordinarily calculated by preparing a *balance sheet* like the one on p. 78. Although it is often difficult to place a value on certain items, like household goods, an attempt should be made to estimate as accurately as possible their current value if they were to be sold.

Leonard and Delores Baxter
Balance Sheet

Assets

Cash in the checkbook	$ 550	
Cash in savings	18,000	
Cash value of life insurance	4,500	
Investments in stock	5,000	
Household goods (Estimated)	20,000	
Automobile (Estimated)	7,000	
Total Assets		$55,050

Liabilities

United Bank (Auto Loan)	$ 8,000	
Mastercard	600	
Sears charge card	500	
Total Liabilities		$ 9,100

Net Worth

Leonard and Delores Baxter, Capital	$45,950
Total Liabilities and Net Worth	$55,050

The amount of the prospect's net worth is of great importance since it shows the prospect's financial strength. A prospect with a high net worth compared to the sale price of your home will probably be able to make the financial arrangements necessary to make the purchase. This is often true regardless of the amount of cash the prospect currently has on hand.

Cash Available

Although a prospect may not wish to share his or her balance sheet information with you, it would not be out of line for you to ask how much cash the prospect will have available to put toward the purchase of the home.

The amount of cash available may be as important as the prospect's net worth. Obviously, the more cash your prospect can come up with, the easier it will be for your prospect to make the purchase, or to obtain a loan if that is necessary.

Many people may overlook ready sources of cash, and it may be necessary for you to recommend that your prospect consider one or more of the following:

1. Life insurance cash value. Permanent life insurance policies (whole life, limited-payment life, annuity, endowment, etc.) build up a cash value. This may be borrowed by the policy owner, ordinarily at very low interest rates. An advantage of borrowing the cash value is that it *never* has to be repaid; the policy owner only has to pay annual interest. Of course, if the insured dies, the proceeds of the policy are decreased by the amount of cash value that was borrowed.

2. Investments in stocks or bonds. An investor may find that selling stocks, bonds, and other investment securities and investing the proceeds in a home will yield a greater rate of return than is currently earned.

3. Loans from relatives. Many people, particularly the young, may be able to obtain a personal loan from their parents or another close relative to aid in the purchase of their home.

Some people will refuse to consider this avenue, but others will try it without hesitation.

4. Sale of unnecessary assets. Some people may be able to turn some of their extra assets into cash. A family

with two cars, two snowmobiles, two motorcycles, and a boat may willingly exchange some of these items for a home of their own.

Income

The easiest, most worry-free way to sell a home is to find a buyer who has the cash. Unfortunately, most buyers do not have sufficient cash, and therefore some type of financing must be arranged. It's at this point that the buyer's income becomes important. Lenders must be convinced that the buyer will have sufficient income to pay all of their living expenses and be able to make monthly loan payments as well before a loan will be granted.

In evaluating income, the combined income of a husband and wife (or other cobuyers) is considered. Also, reliable and stable income from outside sources, such as a second job, is included. Public-assistance income cannot be excluded by the lender.

Evaluation procedures vary somewhat from lender to lender, and it's difficult to state a precise formula that's universally used. Also, variations will exist depending upon an individual borrower's personal circumstances.

Even though this is the case, the following formula can be used as a general guideline to determine the amount of the borrower's monthly income that can be devoted to home payments. (Note: It should be pointed out that some of the rules of thumb used by some people to estimate the purchase price a buyer could afford are not necessarily accurate, particularly when interest rates are high. These include the guideline "You can purchase a home that is two or two and one-half times your annual income," and, "Twenty-five percent of your monthly income can go toward monthly payments for principal and interest.")

Most lenders will allow a borrower to apply 36%–38%

of *gross* monthly income to all debt payments. This includes the monthly payment for principal and interest on the real estate loan, $1/12$ of the annual real estate taxes, $1/12$ of the annual homeowner's insurance premium, *and* any other loan payments the borrower currently has. This is illustrated in the following example:

Leonard and Delores Baxter's combined annual income is $36,000. Therefore, their gross monthly income is $3,000 ($36,000 ÷ 12). If 38% is allowed for all debt payments, the Baxters can allocate $1,140 per month ($3,000 × 38%).

The $1,140 is the amount that can be spent on *all* debt payments. The Baxters currently have a $8,000 auto loan on which the payment is $250 per month and have charge account balances totaling $1,100 on which monthly payments total $110. The total of these monthly payments ($360) must be deducted to determine the amount that is available to apply monthly toward the purchase of a home.

$1,140	Total available monthly for all debt payments
− 360	Current monthly debt payments
$ 780	Available monthly for home purchase

If the real estate taxes on your home are $1,200 per year ($100 per month) and the insurance is $480 per year ($40 per month), these must be deducted to determine the amount that can be allocated toward the monthly loan payment.

$780	Available monthly for home purchase
− 140	Monthly amount for real estate taxes and insurance
$640	Available for monthly home loan payments

It has now been determined that the Baxters can pay (approximately) $640 per month for their loan payment. The amount of loan that the Baxters can obtain with their

$640 per month depends upon two factors: (1) The rate of interest, and (2) The length of the loan.

The higher the rate of interest, the lower the amount that can be borrowed for their $640 per month; the lower the rate, the more that can be borrowed. The longer the length of the loan, the more that can be borrowed; the shorter the length of the loan, the lower the amount that can be borrowed.

Therefore, the maximum loan amount the Baxters can obtain will result from getting as low an interest rate as possible and from getting the loan for as many years as possible.

Lending institutions set their own rates of interest and the borrower can do little to change that. Most lenders are somewhat flexible in the number of years for which they will grant a real estate loan, with 15, 20, 25, and 30 years being normal.

The table on page 83 shows the amount of monthly payment required to amortize (repay) loans at selected interest rates and repayment periods.

If the current interest rate is 11% and the Baxters obtain a loan for 25 years, it can be seen from the loan payment table that their $640 per month would allow them to borrow between $65,000 and $70,000, probably around $65,500.

Therefore, if the home is priced at $89,500 and the Baxters can borrow $66,500, they will need a cash down payment of $24,000 ($89,500 − $65,500).

Although the figures in the foregoing example are not precise, they give a good indication of whether or not the prospect's financial capabilities are in the "ballpark."

If the prospect's finances fall far short of what will be required to purchase your home, and if there's no way of making an immediate improvement, the prospect is not

LOAN PAYMENT TABLE

Amount of Loan	9% Years 20	25	10% Years 20	25	11% Years 20	25	12% Years 20	25
$ 20,000	$ 179.95	$ 167.84	$ 193.01	$ 181.75	$ 206.44	$ 196.03	$ 220.22	$ 210.65
30,000	269.92	251.76	289.51	272.62	309.66	294.04	330.33	315.97
40,000	359.90	335.68	386.01	363.49	412.88	392.05	440.44	421.29
45,000	404.88	377.64	434.26	408.92	464.49	441.06	495.49	473.96
50,000	449.87	419.60	482.52	454.36	516.10	490.06	550.55	526.62
55,000	494.85	461.56	530.77	499.79	567.71	539.07	605.60	579.28
60,000	539.84	503.52	579.02	545.23	619.32	588.07	660.66	631.94
65,000	584.83	545.48	627.27	590.66	670.93	637.08	715.71	684.60
70,000	629.81	587.44	675.52	636.10	722.54	686.08	770.77	737.26
75,000	674.80	629.40	723.77	681.53	774.15	735.09	825.82	789.92
80,000	719.79	671.36	772.02	726.97	825.76	784.10	880.87	842.58
85,000	764.77	713.32	820.27	772.40	877.37	833.10	935.93	895.25
90,000	809.76	755.28	868.52	817.84	928.97	882.11	990.98	947.91
95,000	854.74	797.24	916.78	863.27	980.58	931.11	1,046.04	1,000.57
100,000	899.73	839.20	965.03	908.71	1,032.19	980.12	1,101.09	1,053.23
200,000	1,799.45	1,678.39	1,930.02	1,817.41	2,064.37	1,960.23	2,202.17	2,106.45
300,000	2,699.17	2,517.58	2,895.07	2,726.11	3,096.55	2,940.35	3,303.25	3,159.67

qualified. On the other hand, if the prospect's finances seem to be a little short of what they should be, this prospect may well be worth working with since there may be ways to put the deal together.

Complete interest tables are available at bookstores. A current table showing loan amounts in thousand-dollar increments and at all commonly quoted interest rates may be worth purchasing.

Familiarize yourself with interest rates and repayment periods used by various lenders in your area. You can then intelligently determine with your prospect the amount of monthly payment required to repay a loan. Since interest rates change frequently, you should check every week or two to keep abreast of current rates.

Restructuring Loan Payments

The prospective buyer can often "find" more money to apply toward their monthly home loan payments by restructuring their loan payment schedules on existing consumer loans. In the following example, the Baxters had loans and loan payments as shown below:

	Amount	Monthly Payment
Loan on automobile:	$8,000	$250
Charge account balances:	1,100	110
Totals:	$9,100	$360

It may be possible for the Baxters to obtain a new loan to pay off their auto loan and their charge account balances. This new loan would be for the total of their existing loans, $9,100. If it is set up with a long repayment period, it should decrease their monthly payments considerably.

If, for instance, the new loan payments were $240 per

month, the Baxters would free up $120 ($360 − $240) more per month to apply toward their home loan payments. This would increase the amount that can be borrowed by approximately $12,000. So, instead of being able to borrow only $65,500, the Baxters could now borrow about $77,500 for the home loan. In many cases, this type of loan restructuring makes the difference in determining if a buyer can make the purchase of a home or not.

Since loan officers often overlook the possibility of restructuring a borrower's present loan payments, you may need to make this suggestion to your prospect.

Increasing Income

Often, the one-income family does not earn enough to afford them many of the things they would like to have. If the family's income is not high enough to qualify for a loan on your home, that income can be increased by the spouse's going to work or by "moonlighting." Many people have found this to be the ideal solution, or the only one, that enables them to purchase their dream house. This, of course, is a decision that the prospects need to make after weighing all of the possible repercussions, but it may be worth suggesting.

Many lenders require that a worker demonstrate job stability of 2 or 3 months' employment before they will recognize the income from that job as applying toward the applicant's loan qualification. If you can wait that long to complete the sale of your home, it may be an ideal way to help the buyer get qualified.

Character

The term *character* is difficult to define with exactness. When lenders evaluate a prospective borrower, however, it is one of the main factors they consider.

In general terms, to a lender, character means this: "Is this borrower the type of person who wants to and will try his or her best to repay this loan according to their loan agreement?" If the answer to this question is *yes*, and if the prospect qualifies financially, the lender will make the loan. If the answer is *no*, regardless of the prospect's financial position, the loan probably will be turned down.

What this means from your viewpoint in selling your home is this: If you are dealing with someone of known questionable character, there is a good possibility that their loan application will not be successful. Therefore, you should proceed cautiously. Likewise, you should be careful in entering into any agreement with this type of person lest they attempt to take advantage of you or treat you unfairly. Since you own the home and are selling it yourself, you may refuse to deal with anyone you choose if you feel their financial abilities or character are questionable.

11

How the Buyer's Financing Will Affect You

Many buyers will not have sufficient funds to make a cash purchase and will thus need to rely on some type of financing. There are many types of financing plans that the buyer might attempt to use. It is important that you as seller have a basic understanding of how these plans operate for two reasons:

1. You can suggest a particular type of lender to the buyer. This might be particularly important if certain lenders are temporarily not making loans, or if the buyer is turned down on a loan application from the first lender approached.
2. Some types of lenders require the *seller* to make a cash payment so that the buyer can get a loan, or they require the seller to make substantial improvements to the property before a loan will be granted to the buyer. It is important that you be aware of these possibilities

before you agree that you will make the sale based on the buyer's obtaining financing from one of these lenders.

TYPES OF FINANCING

Economic conditions on a national and local scale affect the availability of money from lenders for financing the purchase of a home. During some periods, some lenders are not interested in or able to make loans, and the buyer will need to "hunt" for a source of financing. Since your goal is to sell your home, it will be in your best interests to work with the buyer in exploring every possibility for obtaining that financing.

It is not unusual for a buyer to be turned down on a loan application from one lender and to then subsequently obtain the loan elsewhere. This means that if your prospective buyer appears to be qualified, you may need to encourage the buyer to make a second or even a third loan application if the initial application is turned down. Some potential types of financing for you to consider are described below. In each case, the buyer will need to present a written copy of the purchase agreement before the lender will begin processing the loan application.

Conventional Loan

A *conventional loan* is the "regular" home loan granted by a Savings and Loan Association, Mutual Savings Bank, commercial bank, or similar lender. Savings and Loans are the most predominent lenders in this market.

Usually, the lender will not, or cannot, loan more than 80% of the purchase price. Therefore, if your sales price is $85,000, the lender will loan a maximum of $68,000 ($85,000 × 80%). The buyer will need to come up with the remainder, $17,000, in cash or through some other arrangement with you.

Interest rates are set by Savings and Loans and other lenders according to their costs of obtaining funds and prevailing rates charged by competitors. Since rates may vary slightly (perhaps 1/8% to 1/2%) from one lender to another, the buyer may be well advised to make a telephone inquiry before making a formal loan application.

Conventional Loans Guaranteed by Private Mortgage Insurance

Although conventional loans ordinarily require a 20% down payment of the purchase price, conventional loans guaranteed by private mortgage insurance may be obtained from Savings and Loans and other lenders for as little as 5% down. The loan is then insured by a private mortgage company.

Basically, the borrower must meet the same requirements as when applying for a conventional loan, and the interest rate is the same as on conventional loans. The borrower must, in addition, pay the private mortgage insurance premium. The amount of premium varies with the length of the loan and the percent of down payment made. The premium charged in the first year is higher than that charged in following years as shown in the following chart for a 30-year loan.

Down Payment Made (Percent of Loan)	First Year Insurance Premium (Percent of Loan)	Following Years Insurance Premium (Percent of Loan)
5%–10%	1.10%	.50%
10%–15%	.65%	.35%
15%–19%	.50%	.35%

For example, if a borrower made an 8% down payment and borrowed $50,000, the first year's insurance premium would be $550 (1.10% of $50,000). Each year after that, the premium would be $225 (.50% of $50,000).

If a borrower made a 12% down payment and borrowed $50,000, the first year's insurance premium would be $325 (.65% of $50,000). In following years, the premium would be $175 (.35% of $50,000).

The first year's insurance premium is ordinarily payable in advance, and thereafter $1/12$ of the next year's annual premium can be included in the borrower's monthly payments.

When the borrower's equity in the property reaches 20% of the market value (through inflation and decrease in the loan's principal), the lender may waive the necessity of carrying the insurance any longer.

Veteran's Administration (VA) Loans

Veteran's Administration loans are made by local lenders (Savings and Loans, etc.) and are guaranteed by the U.S. Veteran's Administration. Veterans of World War II, the Korean War, and the Vietnam Conflict may be eligible.

The VA loan does not ordinarily require a down payment from the borrower, and the borrower does not pay an insurance premium for the VA guarantee. The lender follows the same guidelines used for extending conventional loans when determining a borrower's financial eligibility.

Interest rates on VA loans are set by the Veteran's Administration and are ordinarily lower than rates on conventional loans. Since the VA loans are made by local lenders, and since the interest rates are lower than conventional loans made by the same lenders, the local lender will not earn a satisfactory rate of interest by making VA loans at the interest rate allowed by the

Veteran's Administration. Therefore, to compensate for receiving a lower rate of interest on a VA loan, the lender requires receipt of a cash payment at the time a VA loan is made.

The amount of cash payment required is determined by the spread between VA loan interest rates and conventional interest rates. If there is very little difference between the two rates, a small cash payment is required. If a wide spread exists, a large cash payment will be necessary. The amount of cash payment required is stated in terms of *discount points*. Each discount point represents a percentage point that is multiplied times the amount borrowed to determine the amount of cash payment.

For example, assume that the conventional interest rate is 11% and the VA rate is 10.50% and that 4 discount points will be assessed. If the borrower has applied for a $50,000 loan, this means a $2,000 cash payment ($50,000 × 4%) must be made in order to obtain the VA loan.

In essence, the local lender says to the borrower, "I will loan the $50,000 to you under one of the following two plans:

   a. a conventional loan at 11% interest; or,
   b. a VA loan at 10.5% interest plus $2,000 cash in advance."

The borrower (buyer) is prohibited from paying discount points on a VA loan, so they must be paid by the *seller*. Therefore, in order for the buyer to obtain the VA loan, *you* as seller would have to pay the local lender making the loan a cash payment of $2,000. For this reason, sellers are often reluctant to sell to a buyer who plans to obtain a VA-guaranteed loan.

Often, however, the seller compensates for the discount points that must be paid by refusing to negotiate to a lower sales price, which otherwise might be the case if the buyer were obtaining a conventional loan that would not require the seller to make a cash payment for discount points.

For example: If the asking price on the seller's home is $89,500, the seller might be willing to negotiate to $86,000 for a cash sale or for one involving conventional financing. If the buyer were to obtain VA financing, which would require the seller to pay discount points, the seller might stand firm on the $89,500 price. In this way, the buyer indirectly pays the discount points by paying a higher price for the property.

With a VA loan, the borrower is required to pay the VA a 1% *funding fee* and also may be charged a *loan origination* fee not to exceed 1% of the loan amount.

Your local Savings and Loan Association will be able to tell you the interest rates on VA loans and the exact number of discount points and other charges that will be assessed to the buyer and to the seller. Since these interest rates and the number of discount points may change frequently, you will need to check immediately before agreeing to a sale that involves a VA guaranteed loan.

Even though VA-guaranteed loans involve a certain degree of hassle, they should not be overlooked as a viable method of financing the sale. When conventional loans are difficult to obtain, VA loans may be still available.

(Note: Make certain you also pay special attention to the section on "Lender-Required Repairs" on page 102.)

Federal Housing Administration (FHA) Loans

Federal Housing Administration loans are very similar to VA loans because they are made by local lenders and are insured by FHA. The borrower is required to make a down payment when obtaining an FHA-insured loan. The amount of down payment is determined by applying a sliding scale, but the amount averages less than 5% of the purchase price.

The Federal Housing Administration sets the rate of interest charged by local lenders on FHA-insured loans. As with VA-guaranteed loans, this rate is ordinarily lower than that charged on conventional loans. Therefore, the lender compensates for receiving this lower interest rate by charging discount points as is done for the VA-guaranteed loans described above. With a FHA loan, however, the discount points can be paid by *either* the buyer or the seller, with no more than 5 points paid by the seller. Within this limitation, the buyer and seller negotiate who will pay the discount points.

A one-time FHA mortgage insurance premium must be paid when the loan is obtained. This can be paid by the buyer or the seller, or it can be added to the loan balance. The buyer may also be charged a loan origination fee of 1% of the amount borrowed.

FHA loans are ordinarily more difficult for a borrower to qualify for and to obtain than VA loans.

(Note: Make certain you also pay special attention to the section on "Lender-Required Repairs" on page 102.)

Farmers Home Administration (FmHA) Loans

The Farmers Home Administration is an agency of the U.S. Department of Agriculture and makes direct loans to borrowers. These loans are for property located in rural areas or in communities of 10,000 or less located outside of urban areas. Under certain circumstances, communities of 10,000–20,000 population may also qualify.

FmHA loans are designed to help low and moderate income persons purchase a home that is modest in size, design, and cost. The maximum family income varies from county to county, but it may be possible for a family earning as much as $20,000 or more to qualify.

This is particularly true if there is a large number of dependent children in the household.

A Farmers Home Administration loan does not require a down payment from the borrower. Loans are granted for up to 33 years and under certain circumstances, up to 38 years. Monthly loan payments are thus very low compared to conventional loan repayment plans. For borrowers with very low incomes, FmHA may subsidize the borrower's interest payments, which makes the borrower's monthly loan payment very low.

A considerable length of time, often four weeks or more, is required for FmHA to determine an applicant's eligibility for its program. Several more weeks may be required after that for an appraisal of your home and for possession before the sale can be completed.

It should be mentioned that many persons confuse the Federal Housing Administration, FHA, with the Farmers Home Administration, FmHA, in ordinary conversation. Make certain you clarify which one a prospective buyer is talking about when he or she mentions "FHA."

(Note: Make certain you also pay special attention to the section on "Lender-Required Repairs" on page 102.)

State or Local Finance Plans

From time to time, states or even cities, have devised finance plans to make money available to buyers in their area. These plans may be available to everyone, or they may be just for first-time buyers or for persons moving into the community. These plans are usually administered through local lenders or are connected with a governmental agency such as the Federal Housing Administration.

These finance plans usually offer lower interest rates than those prevailing in the general market. Ask your local lenders if any of these funds are currently available or are slated to be offered in the near future.

Credit Union Loans

Most credit unions do not currently make real estate loans; however, be watchful of new developments in this area.

Even though credit unions may not yet be a viable source of real estate loans, they should be considered as a source of loans for the borrower to pay off existing loans, consolidate loans, or borrow extra money needed for a down payment.

Contract For Deed

Under a *contract for deed*, the buyer makes a down payment to the seller and then makes periodic payments of principal and interest directly to the seller over a period of some years. In effect, therefore, the seller fills the role of the lender and no lending institution is involved.

Ordinarily for an owner to be in a position to sell on a contract for deed, the owner must have the property paid for. This is because most lenders have a *due on sale clause* in their mortgages. This means that if the owner has an existing loan on the property, that loan must be paid off first before the owner can sell the property.

An owner should proceed carefully when contemplating a sale on contract for deed. Usually, a substantial down payment should be required of the buyer that firmly obligates the buyer to want to complete the terms of the agreement. Also, the buyer's financial ability to make monthly, quarterly, semiannual, or annual payments must be carefully analyzed.

Often, sales on a contract for deed call for a *balloon payment* in 3, 5, or 10 years. This means that the buyer makes payments over a specified number of years, and then at some designated time in the future, 3, 5, or 10 years hence, the buyer must pay off the balance owed.

Use of a contract for deed can be an excellent way to

sell property when it's difficult for buyers to obtain loans from regular lenders.

Have your attorney or accountant clearly explain all of the ramifications of selling on a contract for deed before you proceed with such an arrangement.

Loan Assumption

If you have an existing loan on your property, particularly if it's at a low interest rate, the buyer may wish to assume that loan. By assuming the loan, the buyer will essentially be substituted in your place on the existing loan and will become responsible for making all future payments.

For example: You and the buyer agree on a sales price of $89,000, and you have an existing loan on the property for $60,000 at 9% interest. If current rates are 12%, the buyer may wish to assume your low interest loan at 9% instead of obtaining a new loan at 12%. The buyer would then pay you $29,000 cash ($89,000 − $60,000) and assume your loan for $60,000 at 9% interest. If your loan is assumable, this can be an excellent selling point.

Unfortunately, not all lenders allow the assumption of existing loans; they would rather make a new loan to the buyer at the current interest rate. Therefore, you should review your loan agreement or check with your lender to see if your loan can be assumed. If your loan is from a commercial bank, chances are good that it is assumable. If you currently have a Veteran's Administration (VA) loan on your property, it can be assumed by anyone, even if they are not a veteran. If you have a FHA loan more than 2 years old on your property, it can be assumed by the buyer without FHA approval.

Although many lenders will not allow existing low interest rate loans to be assumed by the buyer, the lender may be willing to work out a compromise.

For example: If your loan is at 9% and the current rate is at 12%, the lender *may* allow your buyer to assume your loan at a rate between 9% and 12%, perhaps at 11% or 11½%. During periods of high interest rates, this can be very attractive to a buyer, and you should check in advance to determine if your lender will be willing to work out this type of compromise.

Many loan agreements contain a due on sale clause, which says that the owner must pay off an existing loan when the property is sold. If this clause is in your loan, you will be unable to have the buyer assume your loan without your lender's permission.

Purchase Money Mortgage

Many times a buyer is willing to purchase a property but is a little short of down payment money. In a situation like this, you as seller might consider accepting a promissory note from the buyer for a portion of the purchase price. This is called a *purchase money mortgage*.

For example: Assume that you and the buyer agree on a $89,000 price on your home. The buyer has $15,000 cash, and the lender agrees to make an 80% loan, or $71,200. This means that the buyer can pay you $86,200 ($15,000 cash plus $71,200 from the loan) but is still $2,800 short of the $89,000. If you are in a financial position to do so and if the buyer seems to be a good risk, you might take a $2,800 promissory note from the buyer. Ordinarily, this promissory note will call for the payment of interest. Repayment of the promissory note might be made in monthly installments, periodic payments (quarterly, semiannually, or annually), or might be due in a lump sum in 1, 2, 3, 4, or 5 years.

Be convinced that the buyer will be able to pay off the promissory note as agreed before you enter into this type of arrangement. You can protect yourself by filing a second mortgage on the property.

Lease-Purchase

Under a *lease-purchase* arrangement, the buyer takes possession of the home, moves in, and pays rent under a lease arrangement for a limited period, usually 6–18 months. At the end of the lease period, the buyer must purchase the property and make a final settlement on the purchase price.

This arrangement may call for all or part of the monthly payments to apply toward the purchase price.

The lease-purchase arrangement may work well in a situation where the buyer has little or no down payment money and the seller is anxious to get something, anything, going on the sale of the property.

For example: Assume you and the buyer agree on a sales price of $75,000 on your home. Your buyer has only $5,000 cash, which is insufficient down payment to obtain a loan. You agree that the buyer will move into your home and pay you monthly rental payments of $750 for 12 months. All of the rental payments are to apply toward the purchase of the home, and at the end of the 12 months the buyer is to obtain a loan and pay the remaining balance due you.

At the end of the 12 months, the buyer will need to apply for a loan for $61,000 since the monthly payments of $9,000 (12 months at $750) apply to the down payment and the buyer has $5,000 cash to apply. This is illustrated below:

Sales price:		$75,000
Cash available for down payment:	$5,000	
Rent payments apply to down payment:	9,000	
Down payment:		14,000
Amount of loan necessary:		$61,000

Obviously, under the lease-purchase arrangement, you will end up with lower net proceeds from the sale of your home than if you sold for cash. Therefore, the seller usually compensates for this by refusing to negotiate to as low a sales price as would be acceptable if the sale were for cash. In this way, the seller's net proceeds under the lease-purchase arrangement result in about the same amount as would be realized from a cash sale.

You must carefully choose a buyer to whom you will sell on a lease-purchase basis. You must be convinced that the buyer will be able to make monthly payments as agreed, will attempt to complete the purchase in the future as intended, and will be able to obtain adequate financing when the time comes. Also, you must select a buyer who will take good care of the property, since the deal might fall through and you will then get the property back.

In times when loans are difficult to obtain, a lease-purchase may be an ideal way to sell your home, particularly if your only other option is to let the home sit vacant.

Even, if for some reason, the buyer is unable to complete the purchase of the home as intended, you will still have received an adequate rent for that time period.

CREATIVE FINANCING FOR A TOUGH MARKET

In a strong real estate market—a seller's market—there may be several potential buyers for your home within a reasonable time after you place it for sale. If the first potential buyer can't readily obtain financing, perhaps the next one can. And chances are your buyer will be able to utilize one of the more traditional forms of financing, such as obtaining a conventional loan.

In a tough market, however, there will be fewer potential buyers and you may need to exhaust every financing possibility before you give up on a buyer who cannot obtain traditional financing. In other words, you may need to be more creative in helping your buyer find a way to finance the purchase of your home.

If your buyer cannot obtain a conventional loan, for instance, you may need to consider selling on a contract for deed, using a purchase money mortgage, or selling on a lease-purchase arrangement.

These financing methods may present a higher risk for you than selling to a buyer who finances the purchase through one of the more traditional methods. Therefore, even if buyers are hard to come by, don't resort to using one of these financing methods with an unqualified buyer out of desperation. Make certain your buyer is well qualified, that they will be able to honor their commitment to you, and that you are legally protected in case they do default on their payments.

Lender's Appraisal of Your Home

A lending institution contemplating making a loan to the buyer of your home will make a loan appraisal of your home as part of the lending process. The purpose of this appraisal is to determine if the lender's loan is well secured. In other words, if the buyer defaults on his or her loan payments and the lender must repossess the home, can the lender easily sell the home for enough to cover the buyer's remaining loan balance?

If the buyer is making a substantial down payment, say 30%–40% of the purchase price, the lender is loaning only 60%–70% and will most likely have a well-secured loan. In this case, you can expect little problem with the home appraising for its loan amount.

On the other hand, if the lender is loaning 80% or more of the purchase price, the lender must be much more careful. The lender must be certain that the property is actually worth what the buyer is paying. If the buyer is paying more than the home is worth, and borrowing 80% of that amount, the lender's security position is weakened. In general, you can expect that the lender's appraisals will be much more conservative (lower) when the lender is loaning a high percent of the purchase price.

It may happen that the lender will fail to appraise the home as high as your sales price. For example, assume you and the buyer agree on a sales price of $80,000. The buyer can pay $16,000 down and applies for a $64,000 loan. The lender then appraises the home. The lender's appraised value is $75,000 and the lender refuses to loan the buyer more than $60,000 on its purchase.

You are now faced with a dilemma. You must either accept the lender's appraised value and sell the home at $75,000, or you must convince the buyer that the home is actually worth $80,000. In that case, the buyer will now have to pay you $20,000 cash instead of the $16,000 originally intended, in addition to the $60,000 from the loan. At this point, it will probably be difficult to convince the buyer that the home is worth $80,000 since the lender says it is worth only $75,000.

If the buyer wants the home badly enough, the buyer may come up with the additional down payment necessary to pay you the agreed-on price of $80,000, or the buyer might apply at another lender in the hope of obtaining a higher loan appraisal. Don't count on many buyers being willing to do either of these.

For the buyer's protection, and yours, the written sales agreement will most likely contain a clause that says if the buyer is unable to obtain a loan for the full amount applied for, the buyer is not obligated to purchase the home. Therefore, since your home did not appraise out at the agreed-on sales price, the buyer is no longer obligated to go ahead with the agreement.

If you refuse to accept the lender's appraised amount

and if the buyer refuses to buy at the agreed-on sales price, you must start looking for a different buyer. Your new buyer will have to be in a stronger financial position, with more down payment money than your first buyer, or you'll be undoubtedly faced with the same dilemma all over again.

The fact that your home will most likely be appraised by a lender before a loan will be granted is a good reason for you not to overprice or try to oversell your home. Each home has its own value and somehow the sales price of the home will eventually match that value.

LENDER-REQUIRED REPAIRS

Some lenders, such as Savings and Loan Associations or commercial banks making conventional loans, appraise a home "as is." That is, they appraise it as it stands, with whatever faults and deficiencies there may be, and determine its value in that condition. They ordinarily do not require that any repairs or improvements be made to the home before a loan will be granted.

Those lenders associated with government agencies (Veteran's Administration, Federal Housing Administration, and Farmers Home Administration), however, require that homes meet certain standards before a loan will be granted to the buyer. It's not unusual for the appraiser for one of these lenders to require that the *seller* make numerous improvements to the property. These might include land fill, sodding, rain gutters, downspouts, new stoop, new roofing, new doors, insulation, or many other items. These improvements must ordinarily be paid for by the *seller*.

Caution is therefore recommended before agreeing to sell to a buyer who plans to use one of these financing plans. Allow yourself an escape clause in your contract with the buyer that will allow you to back out of the agreement if these lender-required repairs are excessive.

Even though these lenders may require somewhat costly repairs to be paid by the seller, these lenders still provide a valuable source of financing and should not be overlooked. In some cases, it may well be worth it for you to pay discount points and/or lender-required repairs in order to make the sale of your home.

CHECKING CURRENT LENDING REQUIREMENTS

The preceding information on lender's requirements and procedures is current today, but it may not be tomorrow. With the widely fluctuating interest rates experienced in recent years, lenders have often changed their requirements and offerings overnight. Therefore, you must check periodically to determine a lender's current policies and procedures.

ADJUSTABLE-RATE MORTGAGES

In the past, interest rates and monthly payments on home loans remained constant for the life of the loan. If the loan originated at 10% and payments were $486.50 per month, it remained so for the 20- or 25-year life of the loan.

Many lenders now offer loans known as *adjustable-rate mortgages*, *variable-rate mortgages*, or *renegotiable-rate mortgages*. Under these plans, the lender may raise (or lower) the interest rate, and thus the amount of monthly payment on a borrower's loan as rates fluctuate through the life of the loan. Therefore, if the borrower obtains a loan at 11% with monthly payments of $588.07 per month, there is no guarantee that the interest rate or monthly payment will stay at those figures. If current interest rates become higher than 11%, the lender might raise the borrower's interest rate also on that existing loan. It is easy to see that this borrower's monthly payments may soon reach $600 or $650 per month if interest rates escalate substantially.

All types of adjustable-rate mortgages identify in advance how frequently the interest rate is reviewed for raising or lowering. Usually, this is done each year or every 2 or 3 years. There is a limit how much the interest rate can be raised in any single year, such as no more than 2%, and a limit on how much the interest rate can be raised over the life of the loan, such as no more than 5%.

Since adjustable-rate mortgages are very commonly used, you should be aware that lenders will look at a borrower's future ability to pay increased monthly payments as well as their ability to make payments at the current rate. Because of this, it becomes more important than ever to try to deal with well-qualified buyers when selling your home.

12

Estimating Your Proceeds From the Sale

The sale of real estate involves certain costs that must be paid to complete the transaction. Although state law ordinarily does not specify which of these costs must be paid by the seller or the buyer, normal custom prevails. In a tough market, however, as a sales tactic, you might offer to assume some of the normal seller's costs as a final inducement to get the buyer to buy. In the final analysis, it really doesn't matter if you assume some of the normal seller's payments; it is your net proceeds that count.

Several of the calculations involve prorations of prepaid or accrued items. In some cases, the seller may have made a payment in advance (prepayment) for which the buyer will reimburse a portion to the seller. In other cases, costs or expenses may have accumulated (accrued), which the seller has not yet paid and those must be brought up to date.

Normal Seller's Payments

The following payments are ordinarily required to be made by the seller.

Real Estate Tax Proration

Real estate taxes are paid in arrears. That is, the owners' tax payment is made after the tax has been assessed to the property.

The tax year is either on a calendar year (January 1 to December 31), or on a fiscal year (July 1 of one year to June 30 of the following year) basis. In either case, even when an owner has just made the most recently required tax payment, real estate taxes are still in arrears. The seller must then bring the taxes up to date for the buyer. This calculation varies from state to state, but the general principle is the same.

For example: Assume the real estate taxes on your property are $1,200 per year ($100 per month), and that your state's tax year is on the calendar basis, January 1–December 31. You are to close the sale of your home on April 30 of this year.

Your last tax payment of $600 (for 6 months) was made on March 31 of this year. That tax payment was for January 1–June 30 of the *preceding* year. Therefore, as of the date you are selling your home, April 30, real estate taxes are in arrears (not up to date) from July 1 of the preceding year through April 30 of this year. This is a 10-month period. Since your taxes amount to $100 per month, you will need to pay the buyer $1,000 (10 months at $100 per month) to bring the taxes up to date through your last day of possession of the property, April 30.

This procedure is admittedly confusing to understand. Even many real estate salespeople struggle with the concept. Therefore, it's recommended that you contact your

County Treasurer for a thorough explanation of your state's procedures. The Treasurer will be able to calculate for you the exact amount of real estate tax that you will owe the buyer.

If you make a monthly loan payment that includes amounts for real estate taxes and insurance that go into an escrow account, the balance of that account should be closed out by you when your loan is paid off at the sale closing date. The balance of this account may be sufficient to cover most of your real estate tax proration.

Evidence of Title

Customarily, the seller must produce *evidence of good title* to the property. In many states this involves bringing up to date the *abstract of title* or some similar document. The cost will vary with the amount of time required of the abstracting company or other preparer. A range of $100–$200 is likely.

Contract Preparation

Since you are not using a real estate agent, a *contract* between you and the buyer must be drawn by someone. This is a very important document and it must be accurate and complete. Therefore, an attorney should be used. The seller should most likely expect to pay this cost. The cost will vary depending upon how complicated your agreement is and how much of your attorney's time is required; $50–$200 might be expected.

Deed Preparation

The *deed* must be prepared and delivered to the buyer. An attorney should prepare the deed since it is an extremely important document. The charge for this is minimal, usually $10–$25.

Transfer Tax

Most states require that a transfer tax, also called a *documentary fee*, or *revenue stamps*, be paid on the transfer of real estate at the time the deed is recorded. This fee varies from state to state, but a fee in the range of one-tenth of one percent (.001) to one-fifth of one percent (.002) of the sales price is common. Therefore, if your home sold for $90,000 and the transfer tax in your state is one-tenth of one percent, the transfer tax would be $90 ($90,000 × .001).

Check with your County Recorder to determine your state's transfer tax requirement.

Special Assessments

If a special assessment has been levied against your property for street repairs, storm sewer, or something similar, this is ordinarily payable in installments over several years. The seller ordinarily pays the current installment and the buyer assumes responsibility to pay future installments. This is, however, a negotiable item, and the buyer may insist that the seller pay the entire cost.

If a special assessment has been levied against your property, you have no doubt been made aware of it by your city or county. If you care to double-check, you can contact the County Assessor and the City Clerk's office.

Prepaid Rental Income

If the property involves a rental unit, any rent monies are divided between the seller and the buyer. Ordinarily, rent is collected in advance; therefore, you will need to pay the buyer the portion of the current rent that applies to the number of days the buyer will own the property during that period. If the rent is paid at the end of the rental period, the buyer will need to pay you the rent amount that applies to the time you owned the property during the current rental period.

For example: Assume you rent a basement apartment for $300 per month, and that the tenant pays rent in advance on the 15th of the month. If you are closing the sale of your home on the 25th, you are entitled to keep 10 days' rent, and you will pay the remainder to the buyer. Thus, in a 30-day month, you will keep 10/30, or $100, and pay the buyer 20/30, or $200, of the rental income.

If a *security deposit* had been collected from the tenant by the seller, this is to be paid to the buyer.

Loan Balance And Accrued Interest

If you have a loan on your home, it will most likely need to be paid off from your proceeds on the sale closing date. Your lender can calculate the exact amount owed.

Each monthly loan payment you make consists partly of interest that has accumulated since the last payment was made. Therefore, you will also owe interest on the loan from the date your last monthly payment was made.

Liens Against the Property

If *liens* have been filed against your property, these must be paid off before you will be able to transfer good title.

The most common type of lien is that filed by a lender (a *mortgage*) when a loan is obtained to buy the property. Other liens may be for real estate taxes or for work done on the property by contractors, carpenters, plumbers, or others (*mechanic's liens*) that you have not paid.

Loan Prepayment Penalty

Some loan contracts contain a *prepayment penalty clause*. This states that if a borrower pays off the loan before its maturity, the borrower *may* be assessed a penalty. This penalty varies, but 1% to 1½% of the remaining loan balance is a common range. Thus, if your existing loan balance is $30,000 and a 1% penalty is charged, you may be required to pay the lender $300 for the privilege of paying off your loan.

Even though the lender is entitled to charge this penalty, many do not. Check with your lender to see if the penalty will be assessed.

Survey

Usually, when a house and lot in a residential area is sold, a *survey* is not necessary. Ordinarily, if the buyer requires a survey of the property, the buyer must pay for it.

In some situations, however, it may be the seller's responsibility to pay for a survey. This would ordinarily be the case if the seller divides off a parcel of land from a larger piece and needs to supply an accurate legal description of the parcel being sold.

Survey costs can run from perhaps as low as $100 into the thousands, depending on the amount of time required by the surveyor.

Attorney's Fees

Any legal work done specifically on the seller's behalf is paid for by the seller. Ordinarily, there are few attorney's fees in addition to those already listed above.

Real Estate Commission

Usually, the single largest seller's expense in selling a home is the real estate commission. This normally ranges from 6%–8% of the sales price. If you sell your home your-self, you will not have this charge. If you resort to the use of a real estate company, you must then pay this fee.

If your home were sold for $90,000 and a real estate commission of 7% is charged, the fee would be $6,300. That's a lot of incentive to sell your own home!

Regardless of whether you use the services of a real estate company or not, you will still incur virtually all of the seller's costs identified above.

NORMAL BUYER'S PAYMENTS

The following payments ordinarily must be made by the buyer.

Loan Origination Fees

If the buyer applies for a loan, all costs of obtaining that loan are expenses to the buyer.

Many lenders charge a loan origination fee that covers the lender's cost of establishing the loan. This may vary, but 1% to 2% of the amount borrowed is a common range. Therefore, if the buyer borrows $75,000 and is assessed a 1% loan origination fee, the buyer must pay the lender $750.

Property Appraisal Fee

If the buyer applies for a loan, part of the lender's evalua-tion procedure includes an appraisal of the property being purchased. The buyer must pay for this. The cost will vary, but a range of $100–$200 is normal.

Credit Report

If the buyer applies for a loan, the lender will usually require that the buyer pay for a credit investigation on the buyer's background. This charge might range from $25–$100.

Attorney's Fees

Usually, the buyer will need to rely on an attorney to determine whether or not the seller is delivering good and merchantable title to the property. A charge of $50–$150 is normal.

Proration of Homeowner's Insurance Premium

Premiums for homeowner's insurance are ordinarily paid in advance. The seller will, no doubt, have this insurance in effect on the sale closing date, and the buyer may wish to assume the policy. Since the seller has paid the insurance premium in advance, the buyer must reimburse the seller for the unused portion of the policy.

For example: Assume that on March 1, the seller paid a 1-year premium of $480 ($40 per month). If the sale closing date is April 30, 2 months will have passed since the premium was paid and 10-months' premium is prepaid. The buyer will therefore reimburse the seller for 10-months' premium, or $400.

An insurance policy cannot be assigned without the insurance company's permission, so you will need to check with your agent in advance. Ordinarily, the insurance company will allow this assumption.

If the buyer prefers to secure his or her own insurance from their own agent, they will need to pay the cost of this in advance.

It is beneficial for the seller to have the buyer assume the policy and make a reimbursement for prepaid premium as described above. In this way, the seller gets reimbursed for the full unused portion of the policy that is prepaid. On the other hand, if you cancel your policy, the insurance company will calculate your refund according to a *short rate scale*, and you will receive less than a full refund for the remaining unused portion of the policy.

Recording Fees

In order to give notice to the world that title to the property has transferred, the buyer should record the deed or contract for deed at the county courthouse. The charge for this is minimal, usually $2–$15.

Survey

If a survey is not required of the seller in order to establish a legal description or to identify a disputed boundary, and if the buyer requests a survey for his or her own curiosity, the buyer should expect to pay for the survey. Normally, with residential property, a survey is not necessary. Most likely, the property was surveyed when the home was built and the surveyor placed metal stakes in the ground marking the corners of the lot. Probably the stakes are under the surface, but they can be located with a metal detector.

The cost of a survey may range from as little as $100 to several thousand dollars, depending upon the amount of time required of the surveyor.

Utilities Deposits

If deposits are required in your community for electricity, water, sewer, natural gas, telephone, TV cable, and other utilities, it's the buyer's obligation to pay these deposits. If the utility companies will allow it, the seller's deposits can be transferred to the buyer's name, and the buyer can reimburse the seller on the sale closing date.

Estimating Your Proceeds

The amount of proceeds from the sale of your property can be established by completing a worksheet like the one illustrated below. Even though you may not have

Seller's Proceeds

	Payments	Receipts
Receipts		
Sales price		_____
Insurance premium proration		_____
Other: _____		_____
Other: _____		_____
Total Receipts		_____
Payments		
Real estate tax proration	_____	
Evidence of title (Abstracting, etc.)	_____	
Contract preparation	_____	
Deed preparation	_____	
Transfer tax	_____	
Special assessments	_____	
Proration of prepaid rental income	_____	
Balance of loan	_____	
Interest on loan since last payment	_____	
Loan prepayment penalty	_____	
Liens on property	_____	
Attorney's fees	_____	
Survey	_____	
Other: _____	_____	
Other: _____	_____	
Total Payments		_____
Net Proceeds (Total Receipts less Total Payments)		_____

exact amounts available, you can probably estimate closely enough to give a good indication of what your net proceeds will be.

Completion of this worksheet can be very helpful when setting your asking price since it will show you the one amount that's of most interest—the amount of cash you will end up with after the sale is completed.

ESTIMATING BUYER'S CASH REQUIREMENTS

It may be necessary for you to work with the buyer in determining the amount of cash the buyer will need to have available to be able to complete the purchase.

The following worksheet includes receipts the buyer will receive from you for tax prorations and so forth. These will decrease the amount of cash the buyer will need to come up with from his or her own sources.

BUYER'S CASH REQUIREMENTS

	Receipts	Payments
Payments		
Down payment (or cash payment for property)		_____
Loan-origination fees		_____
Property appraisal fee		_____
Credit report		_____
Attorney's fees		_____
Homeowner's insurance premium		_____
Recording fees		_____
Utility deposits		_____
Other: _____		_____
Other: _____		_____
Other: _____		_____
Total Payments		══════

	Receipts	Payments
Receipts		
Real estate tax proration	_____	
Prorated rental income	_____	
Other: _____	_____	
Other: _____	_____	
Other: _____	_____	
Total Receipts		_____
Total Cash Required		
(Total Payments less Total Receipts)		========

The buyer may need hundreds or even thousands of dollars in addition to the cash down payment. Use of the preceding worksheet will help identify those additional costs and will help you to better qualify the buyer.

13

Showing Your Home

Let's assume you have now located someone who is interested in buying your home. An appointment has been made (or the prospect just dropped in) and you're about to begin your face-to-face salesmanship. It goes without saying that this is an important step. Your attitude, manner, and technique should be well prepared so you give a professional showing of your property.

HOME-SHOWING TECHNIQUES

Follow the suggestions below when showing your home to prospects:

1. Before even running your first ad or talking to your first prospect, carefully plan a tour route that will best and most logically display your home. Start in a room that will give an immediate favorable first impression.

Make note of specific features you want to point out in your home, and work at developing the proper wording to describe them.

ADDRESS: 1606 Danburry Heights
OWNERS: Steven and Julie Gibbs
TELEPHONE: 217-555-5740
TYPE HOUSE: Ranch
LOT SIZE: 80′ × 150′

PHOTOGRAPH
OF HOME

EXTERIOR: Vinyl Siding, 40-year guarantee
ROOF: Asphalt
SQUARE FEET: 1,500 square feet (30′ × 50′) plus garage
AGE OF HOME: Built in 1986
INSULATION: R16 sidewalls, R36 attic
HEAT: Natural gas, forced air furnace
CENTRAL AIR-CONDITIONING: Electric
COST OF HEAT: Average $70 per month (past 12 months)
WATER HEATER: 40 gallons, natural gas
KITCHEN CABINETS: Oak veneer
WOODWORK: Solid Oak
KITCHEN SINK: Double, stainless steel
BASEMENT: Full with finished recreation room (20′ × 26′) and half bath
GARAGE: Double (22′ × 24′)
DRIVEWAY: Concrete
REAL ESTATE TAXES: $1,887.82 (after homestead exemption)

Room Sizes
Kitchen: 14′ × 16′
Dining Room: 10′ × 12′
Living Room: 14′ × 22′
Den: 10′ × 14′
Master Bedroom: 16′ × 18′
Bedroom: 12′ × 14′
Bedroom: 10′ × 12′
Utility Room: 6′ × 10′
Master Bathroom: 8′ × 12′
Bathroom: 6′ × 8′

Special Features
• Garbage disposal
• 220 electric in kitchen and garage
• Combination windows
• Built-in dishwasher
• 2 electric garage door openers
• All drapes and curtains stay with house
EXCLUDE: storage shed in back yard

POSSESSION DATE: 30 days' notice preferred

2. Practice giving your tour to your spouse or a friend until you feel at ease and have your planned presentation down to perfection.

3. Develop an information sheet, like the one shown on page 118, that you can hand to your prospect. This can be easily duplicated on a copy machine, offset, or mimeograph by a friend who works in an office or school.

A well-prepared information sheet will answer many unasked questions the prospect may have, and will serve as a handy guide for you so that you don't miss anything. It will also serve as an accurate reminder for your prospects when they later reflect on your home. (Note: You may wish to leave the price off the printed sheet since you may not want to discuss price with your prospect until after you have shown them the home.)

4. Make sure your home looks its best and smells its best. Home-baked bread or fresh-cut flowers (from your own flower garden) give a wonderful, homey aroma that will make a favorable impression on your prospect's senses.

5. Put house pets that snarl, hiss, or growl outdoors.

6. Do not have blaring sound systems or television sets on that will interfere with communication and concentration. Soft music, however, may help to take the edge off the silence between conversation and may help to make your prospect feel relaxed and at ease in your home.

7. Have family members routinely go about their tasks.

8. Display a friendly nature. The prospect is not your enemy—selling a home is not a war. If you treat prospects in a friendly, sincere manner, they will react to you in the same way.

9. Do not let your emotions get involved—relax. Yes, it may be the home where you raised your family, and it may hold many fond memories. These factors will have

little meaning to your prospects since they aren't buying your memories; they are buying your home.

Try to remain emotionally detached and unbiased as you speak of and show your home.

10. Don't let it show how much it means to you to sell your home. Don't grovel or beg.

11. Ask the buyer some questions before you start the full showing of the home to determine the prospect's needs (family size, etc.) and wants. Continue to ask questions as you show the home to check your prospect's "temperature."

12. Listen to what the prospect says and to what the prospect does not say. Watch for body language that indicates how the prospect is thinking. The way a prospect longingly admires a feature, touches something, or gives a knowing look to a companion might tell you more than words could.

13. Keep in mind the buyer's needs, wants, and strongest buying motives. Try to appeal to them by matching your home's features and advantages to those needs, wants, and motives.

14. The price of any property is relative to what the buyer is getting. Therefore, point out the various benefits, advantages, and features your home has that justify your asking price, although you should not specifically tell your prospect that this is what you're doing.

15. If something is of unusual value or cost, point this out to the prospect and state the amount it cost you. Stand ready to furnish receipts and/or cancelled checks to back up your statements if necessary.

16. Point out features about your home that you have particularly enjoyed and tell why. The prospect might likewise enjoy these features for the same reasons.

17. You can point out minor or seemingly inconsequential features or benefits, but don't dwell on them or overly emphasize them.

18. Have receipts of heating costs available as proof. Your prospects will appreciate your openness and willingness to verify your statements.

19. Be honest. Don't make any statements that are untrue or of which you are uncertain. Don't try to hide any of your home's defects. The prospect will only find out the truth later, anyway, and problems will develop.

20. All prospective buyers, being people, will not act the same way when they view your home. Most will undoubtedly be kind, gracious, and sincere. A few prospects, however, may say seemingly unkind things about your home or about your decorating. Don't let this upset you. Some prospects will only be trying to point out flaws so they will seem justified in trying to lower your price. Others are merely inconsiderate. Try to identify if the prospect's comments are real or sincere, and if so, find an answer or solution to their objection.

21. If possible, have photographs of your home showing it in different seasons of the year. If you're selling your home in the winter, it might be particularly helpful to show photographs taken in spring or summer when the lawn, trees, and flowers are in full bloom.

22. Let your prospect's pace guide you in determining the length of time a showing should take. Some prospects are fast lookers who will want to charge from room to room and finish looking at the home in 5 minutes. Others will scrutinize every feature and detail.

Keep control of the showing and lead the prospects from room to room according to your predetermined plan.

23. When you've finished showing the home, sit your prospects down in a cozy room (one that you have preselected) to discuss their interest in your home.

14

Overcoming Obstacles to the Sale

It's very possible that some prospects may like your home, but for some reason, it may not fit their needs or wants exactly. In some cases, you may be able to make suggestions to the buyer that will overcome those obstacles.

1. Not enough bedrooms. Look for possible ways that more bedrooms can be added by converting other space to bedroom usage. Perhaps the buyer could finish off the attic, enclose a porch, or utilize part of the basement.

2. Too many bedrooms. Some prospects may not need as many bedrooms as your home has. You might point out that extra bedrooms could be utilized for a guest bedroom, home office, sewing room, den, children's play room, music room, or storage room.

3. Master bedroom too small. This is a common complaint since many prospects have huge bedroom sets that will require a large bedroom. Perhaps an interior

wall can be removed, thus converting two small bedrooms into a larger one. Perhaps part of a large closet
can be converted to a bedroom area.

4. Kitchen too small. This is an obstacle that has
stopped many wives from endorsing the purchase of a
home. Regardless of how much they like the rest of the
home, they won't buy it if the kitchen isn't suitable.
Perhaps the kitchen can be made larger by moving or
removing an interior wall. Perhaps an adjoining porch
can be used for storage so there's more usable space in
the kitchen.

5. Not enough bathrooms. Perhaps a porch, pantry, or
closet could be converted. Perhaps an extra bathroom
can be installed in the basement.

6. Heating costs too high. If your heating costs *are* too
high, you cannot prove to the prospect that they aren't.
Therefore, you may need to make an allowance in the
sales price so that the prospect can properly insulate.

7. Colors are wrong. Each buyer has in mind a certain
color combination of carpet, walls, and draperies that
matches their tastes and their present furniture. If the
prospect otherwise likes the home, you might volunteer
to buy the paint so that the prospect can repaint walls to
their liking. If you're receiving an attractive sales price,
you might offer to repaint, recarpet, or buy new drapes
for the buyer in order to put the deal together.

Many buyers may find the foregoing suggestions too
cumbersome or bothersome to attempt. You only need
one buyer, however, and your suggestions may be the
little bit extra needed to convince that one prospect to
buy the home.

15

Asking the Prospect to Buy

It's often difficult to "read" a prospect's true interest in the property. Some prospects that marvel and ohh and ahh over every feature fail to step forth to complete the purchase. Others who seemingly display little interest might eventually buy. Sometimes, the only way to determine a prospect's true interest is to *ask*.

The method used in asking a prospect will vary with your personality and style, the prospect's disposition, the degree of interest already expressed by the prospect, the amount of contact you have had with the prospect, and the present circumstances.

TECHNIQUES TO AVOID

Before we discuss what you should do in asking if the prospect has an interest in buying, let's look at what you should not do.

1. Do not use a high-pressure, hard-sell approach. Most prospects will react negatively to this and will refuse to do business with you.

2. Do not use the old ploy, used by some real estate salespeople and used car dealers: "If you want to buy it, you'd better take it now because there's two other people that are going to make offers tomorrow."

Most prospects will view this as a certain degree of hucksterism and will resent your attempt to manipulate them. No doubt, far more sales have been lost by this technique than have been gained by it.

3. Do not appear desperate to make the sale.

4. Do not start slashing your price in an attempt to stimulate buyer interest.

USING INDIRECT QUESTIONS

Using direct questions such as, "Do you want to buy—yes or no?" should be ordinarily avoided at the beginning. Instead, you should test your prospect's interest through more indirect and nonthreatening questions. These indirect questions will serve the same purpose, and even if the prospect gives a "no" answer to one of them, it's not a refusal to buy the home.

If the indirect questions don't produce a definite enough measure of the prospect's interest, you can then resort to a more direct line of questioning. Whatever you do, make sure, in some form or the other, you do *ask* the prospect to buy.

Ask a series of seemingly inconsequential questions or make statements like those listed below as you show the home. The prospect's answers or reactions will serve as your guide to the amount of interest your prospect has in your property. Listen to your prospect's answers and tone of voice. Watch for facial expressions and body language. Note that most of the following are questions, but they are phrased as statements designed to secure the prospect's agreement.

- "This home has just the right number of bedrooms for you, doesn't it."
- "This would be a handy location for you, wouldn't it."
- "You would get a lot of use out of this family room, wouldn't you."
- "This would be a great neighborhood for your children, wouldn't it."
- "This bedroom will nicely accommodate your king-size bedroom set, won't it."
- "You will enjoy the double garage, won't you."
- "Feel how thick this carpet is."
- "The heating costs are lower than you might expect, aren't they."
- "You would make good use of the recreation room, wouldn't you."
- "This extra bedroom will make a dandy sewing room or home office, won't it."
- "I'm sure your children will enjoy the short walk to school."
- "That automatic garage door opener is a real convenience, isn't it."
- "Your children would be proud to live in this home, wouldn't they."
- "This is a home you can easily afford, isn't it."
- "This home will fit your life-style well, won't it."
- "This home seems to fit you well."
- "Are there any questions or concerns you have about the home?"
- "Would you like to go back and look at any of the rooms a second time?"
- "Will you be obtaining financing to help complete the purchase of a home?"

- "This home holds a great deal of sentimental value for my (spouse) and me, and we want it to go to someone like you who we know will enjoy it and take good care of it."

USING DIRECT QUESTIONS

If your indirect questioning failed to determine your prospect's interest, more direct questions may be appropriate.

- "Do you think this home will be suitable for your needs?"
- "The home seems to fit your needs very well. Is there any reason you are hesitating?"
- "I can understand your not wanting to make a spur-of-the-moment decision; however, this home seems perfect for you. Is there any reason that we can't go ahead?"
- "Will a 30-day possession date be satisfactory with you?"
- "Your friends will sure be surprised if you buy this home, won't they."
- "Buying a home is a big step in anyone's life that should be taken carefully. Let's make a list of all the reasons that you should buy or should not buy this home. This will help clarify your thinking." (Sit down at a table and make out two lists. Undoubtedly, the list why the prospect should buy will be longer and more convincing.)
- "Level with me—what are your thoughts on this home?"
- "You seem to be hesitating, even though I can tell you would really like to buy this home. What is it that's bothering you?"
- "I realize that the two of you won't want to make a

final decision without first discussing it. I'll go into the kitchen and fix us some coffee so you can be alone."
- "How soon will you be able to make a decision?"

Making the Sale

Your goal is not to be a tour guide of your home—it's to close the sale. Everything you do from the first moment you greet the prospect at the door should be directed toward that end. The questions you ask should solicit various responses from your prospect to indicate quite accurately your prospect's interest. If your prospect makes a strong, positive statement, follow it up by steering your prospect toward making the purchase. Statements from your prospect like the following indicate a very strong buyer interest.

- "I've always wanted a home like this."
- "We must be crazy for thinking of buying a home this expensive."
- "What will our friends say?"
- "I just love this kitchen."
- "This home has so much room in it."
- "I've always dreamed of having a recreation room large enough for a pool table."
- "I wonder if we can afford this home."
- "I'll have to check with my banker."
- "When are you planning to move?"
- "This is a great location."

Although you should not high pressure your prospect, you should nudge the prospect to buy *now*. Prospects left to themselves often fail to reach a conclusion. Prospects who "sleep on" their decision often cool off, and it's extremely difficult, if not impossible, to rekindle their interest.

Don't give up without making several attempts to get your prospect to buy. Be tactful so that you don't offend the prospect and kill off any future interest.

Even though your goal is to get the prospect to make a decision to buy now, many prospects will not move that quickly. They will not want to rush into such a major purchase; they will want to check on financing, they will need to consult with relatives or friends, or do a dozen other legitimate things.

Display understanding for your prospect's concerns. Create a pleasant mood so that your prospect will welcome the chance to talk to you about the home again in the future.

Set some definite dates for when you are to check back with the prospect, when the prospect is to check on financing, when the prospect is to return for a second look at the home, and so forth.

Follow up with each prospect who seems to have an interest in your home and keep in contact with them. Inform them of any changes in your asking price, terms of sale, possession date, or any other pertinent information.

Until a bona fide prospect has signed a written agreement to buy your home, it is not sold. Don't halt your sales efforts by assuming that someone who displayed a strong interest will buy. They may—but then again, they may not. Keep each prospect "alive" and "warm" but also continually seek new, prospective buyers.

Even after a prospect has signed an offer to buy, you might keep in mind names of other prospects as potential "backup" buyers if for some reason the deal falls through.

16

Negotiating the Terms of the Sale

Suppose that you have now located a qualified prospect who wants to buy your home, if satisfactory terms can be agreed upon.

Agreement must be reached on several important items, including price, terms of payment, possession date, and identification of which items do and do not stay with the property. Even though you have stated your preference and wants in each of these areas, the buyer may have different ideas. At this point, a certain degree of negotiation will take place.

Your posture at this point is very important. You should be open to the buyer's opinions and try to understand the buyer's position. Maintain a friendly, yet businesslike attitude. Don't become angry if the buyer offers terms that seem unreasonable; remember, you are in the process of negotiating.

As any professional negotiator will tell you, you may not get everything you want when you sit down at the bargaining table. Your goal should be to try to obtain as closely as you can the things that are *most important* to you. In order to obtain those, you may need to be flexible on or even give up some of the things that do not hold as much importance. This is particularly true if it is a buyer's market, and you may need to make a few concessions to close the deal. For example, if you are firm on your asking price, you may need to be flexible on terms of payment or on possession date to be able to obtain the required sales price.

Some suggestions for negotiating various areas of the sales agreement are listed below:

PRICE

Most buyers feel compelled to negotiate on price. Usually, the buyer will offer an amount that is lower than the asking price. At that point, you can do one of three things:

1. Accept it.
2. Flat out reject it.
3. Counteroffer by offering a price that is somewhere between your original asking price and the buyer's offer.

You must proceed carefully here so that you do not chase off an interested buyer. Obviously, the buyer's offer will largely dictate how you should or must proceed.

The following is probably good advice that should guide you: If the buyer's offer is reasonable, if you can live with it, and if it will allow you to go about your future plans—take it. If the offer is absolutely so low that you cannot possibly accept it, then you should counteroffer at a price that you can accept.

It's nice to get all that you can from the sale of your home—you deserve it. However, don't get greedy. The world is full of people who turned down a good, fair, reasonable offer only to be stuck with the home for many months and then eventually, out of desperation, have sold it for thousands of dollars less than the original offer.

If, by chance, the first prospect (or one of the first) who looks at your home wants to buy it, don't assume that if you turn this offer down it doesn't matter since other offers will arrive daily. It's a guessing game—there may be others, or the next good prospect may be 6 months away. If you're lucky enough to have the good fortune to find a solid prospect early in your sales efforts, complete the sale to that prospect if you can, and don't speculate that somebody else might have come along tomorrow who would have paid more.

Obviously, in all cases, if the prospect makes a ridiculously low offer and will not raise their sights to a reasonable price range, you will have to turn the offer down.

Price is ordinarily the most difficult aspect of the contract to reach agreement on. Once there is agreement here, most of the other aspects will be minor.

TERMS OF PAYMENT

There are many ways in which a buyer can pay for the home, including cash payment, obtaining a real estate loan from a lender, contract for deed, and lease-purchase.

You should decide which of these are acceptable to you and which are not. Your opinion may vary depending upon your present circumstances, the economy, market conditions, and the quality of buyer you are dealing with. If the terms of payment are satisfactory, you should by all means agree to them. On the other hand, if the terms are not acceptable, do not agree to something that you will later regret.

If the prospect is sincere in wanting to buy, but the terms of payment present an obstacle, work together in exploring other possibilities that will be agreeable to both of you.

POSSESSION DATE

No doubt you will have a *possession date* in mind that will be ideal for your circumstances. Often, buyers are willing and able to comply with your wishes.

In some cases, however, a different possession date may be mandatory for the buyer in order for the buyer to be interested in your property. In this situation, be flexible. Consider storing your furniture and renting temporarily if necessary. Sure, this is an inconvenience, but it's nothing compared to how you'll be inconvenienced if you miss this opportunity to sell your home and subsequently don't get it sold for months after your ideal possession date.

ITEMS THAT STAY WITH THE PROPERTY

Even though you have clearly identified to the buyer the items that you intend to leave and not leave with the property, the buyer may have other ideas. Flexibility is probably the key here, too.

If it appears that it's of great importance to the buyer that some item be left with the home (a stove or refrigerator, for example), and if you can possibly part with it, you may be best off giving in on that point.

If the item does not appear to be of great importance

to the buyer, but is more or less included in the offer as an afterthought, you can probably negotiate that item away from the buyer.

It's probably appropriate to recall a suggestion made earlier in this book. If you have items of personal property that hold unique or sentimental value for you, remove them before showing your home to a single prospect. This will eliminate the problem of the buyer's wanting it included in the purchase. Not all items can be removed, of course, but those not holding special meaning to you can be easily replaced if necessary by buying a new one from the proceeds of your sale.

PAYMENT OF SALES EXPENSES

Usually, identifying which of the sales expenses are to be paid by the buyer or the seller does not present a problem when entering into a real estate sales agreement. The custom in your state indicates who is to pay what.

In some cases, though, the buyer may not feel it is "fair" that he or she be assessed a certain charge. Or, if it is a soft market, you might consider offering to pay some of the normal seller's costs as a special concession to get the buyer to make an offer.

Agreeing to pay a sales expense that would ordinarily be borne by the buyer may be necessary if the buyer is adamant in his or her opinion, or if it is necessary to put the deal together in a tough real estate market. Keep in mind that your net proceeds from the sale is the only amount that really matters. If you can afford to pay that expense on the buyer's behalf and still end up with a satisfactory amount of cash from the sale, it is suggested you consider doing so.

BUYER'S SPECIAL PROVISIONS

A buyer may include any conditions or stipulations in the offer that he or she wants. Likewise, you as seller can refuse to accept any of these provisions that you want. If these conditions are not agreed upon, however, you do not have a contract to sell your home.

Certain conditions that might be included by a buyer are as follows:

Subject to Obtaining a Loan

If the buyer needs to obtain a real estate loan to be able to purchase the home, it is normal procedure to make the offer subject to the buyer's being granted a loan by a lending institution. This means that if the buyer is granted the loan, the buyer is obligated to purchase the home. If the buyer is turned down for the loan, the buyer is not obligated to buy the home, and the contract expires.

This clause is for the buyer's protection and indirectly for yours as well. Obviously, if the buyer cannot obtain a real estate loan, there's no way the buyer can come up with the money to purchase the home, and you'll be unable to enforce a sale to that prospect, anyway. If the prospect cannot obtain a loan, the agreement with that prospect terminates, and you can immediately seek a new buyer.

You should, therefore, be convinced that the prospect's chances of obtaining a loan are good or you'll be wasting your time and the prospect's as well by having the prospect apply for a loan that will be obviously turned down.

Subject to the Sale of the Buyer's Home

Often a buyer can be located who wants to buy your home, but there is one "small" problem; the buyer has to sell his or her home first before they can buy yours.

In a case like that, the buyer may make an offer on your home subject to the sale of his or her home within a certain period, say 60 days. What this means is that you will take your home off the market for 60 days; if the prospect's home sells within that time period, the prospect is obligated to buy your home. If the 60 days pass and the buyer's home is not sold, the agreement terminates, the buyer has no obligation to you, and you have taken your home off the market for 60 days on a gamble that did not pay off.

Determining whether or not to accept an offer that's subject to the sale of the buyer's home is one of the most perplexing decisions faced by a seller. General market conditions, the apparent saleability of the prospect's home, and the prospect's willingness to sell at a reasonable price are major factors that will influence your decision.

If you're unwilling to accept the risks involved in the above-mentioned situation, you might suggest one of the following variations to the prospect:

1. Accept the buyer's offer with one change: You will be allowed to continue to try to sell your home during the specified time period. If you receive another offer, your first prospect will be given first chance to buy the home, but that prospect must perform within a limited time period, say 48 or 72 hours. This is called a *first right of refusal*. If your first prospect cannot complete their purchase of your home, you are then free to sell it to your second prospect.

2. Sign an agreement to sell your home to the prospect

at a specified price and terms if their home sells before you sell your home to someone else. This will allow you the freedom to attempt to find another buyer, and it does not obligate you to hold your home off the market for your first prospect.

Initially, your prospect may think that either of these two arrangements is unfair. When you explain that the prospect must get his or her home sold first, anyway, before they can purchase your home, they may see your proposal in a different light.

If, after viewing the prospect's home, it appears that the property is unlikely to sell quickly, you may want to avoid signing any agreement that is subject to the sale of that property.

If you accept some form of agreement to sell your home when the prospect's home is sold, it will be to your advantage to help in the sale of the prospect's home. You can give the prospect advice and actively assist by turning over names of prospects you have come in contact with that might be good potential buyers.

Subject to Other Conditions

A buyer might make an offer that is subject to other conditions (subject to securing a job applied for, subject to receiving an anticipated pay raise, subject to winning a pending law suit, and so forth) in addition to those listed above. If that happens, you will need to analyze each individual situation and evaluate it on its own merits.

Accepting an Exchange

If your prospect has a home for sale but wants to buy yours, perhaps you can trade homes. This can be workable in either of the following situations:

1. If you want a different home and your prospect does too, it might be that each's home is just right for the other person.

If you're planning to stay in the same community, you might seek out other sellers who have a home that is attractive to you. Suggest the idea of a trade to them. They may never have thought of it or pursued it, and they may find the idea attractive.

2. Even if you're leaving the community, it may be worthwhile to consider trading your home for a less expensive one. This will allow you to free up some cash and have a home that may be more suitable for renting out until it can be sold.

For example: Assume you have a $125,000 home, and an owner of a $75,000 home wants to buy it. You could trade homes and you would receive the $50,000 difference. You will then end up with a $75,000 home, which can probably be rented out for enough to cover most of your costs of owning that home.

This doesn't solve your problem, but it lessens the severity of it.

Before accepting another home in exchange for yours, be certain that it will be suitable for your needs if you're planning to live in it, or that it's potentially saleable if you plan to resell it.

Negotiating Procedure

Since you're selling the home yourself without the use of a middleman (real estate agent), you will most likely be dealing with the buyer face to face. It's good to keep in mind throughout the negotiations that you're the owner of the property and are therefore in control of its destiny. You don't have to agree to any terms you don't want to. Your goal should be to negotiate in good faith with the prospect until you are both in agreement on a basis for the sale of your home.

17

The Agreement

A contract for the sale of real estate *must* be in writing to be enforceable. This means that if you only have an oral agreement and the buyer fails to perform, you cannot do anything about it.

In addition to being unenforceable, oral agreements are too open to misinterpretation, confusion, or attempts at deceit.

You and the buyer can verbally discuss and agree on terms. This may be necessary to carry on your negotiation. You should then *immediately* have your agreement reduced to writing. Do not draw your own contract or have a friend do it. This contract is much too important to risk a haphazard or incomplete job.

Have your attorney draw the contract, but don't rely on the attorney to provide all of the specific information that you and the buyer have agreed on. You and the buyer will need to furnish that. If you supply the basic information and describe your intent, the attorney will be able to word the provisions in legal and enforceable language. The attorney will also be able to clarify any areas on which you have questions.

Provisions of the Agreement

The written contract between you and the buyer should be complete and should include every detail of your agreement, including the following stipulations:

- Names of the buyer(s) and seller(s). Even if the buyer is married, he or she can buy in their own name without being accompanied by their spouse.

    If you, the seller, are married, your spouse must join in the sale. This is true even if the property is held in your name only, since through marriage your spouse acquires rights that will need to be transferred.
- A proper legal description of the property. This can be obtained from tax records, the abstract, or from the county courthouse.
- A list of all personal property and fixtures that are included in the sale. If there are any items that might be questionable but are to be excluded from the sale, they should be specifically stated as such.
- A description of the method of payment. This includes the amount of down payment, financing to be applied for, loan assumptions, and so forth.
- The date of possession and date of closing.
- A statement that real estate taxes are to be prorated to the date of possession.
- A statement designating who will pay special assessments, if there are any.
- A statement identifying any proration of rents, rent deposits, homeowner's insurance premium, and the like.
- A statement of the amount of *earnest money* to be paid by the buyer at the time the agreement is signed. This is a cash payment that demonstrates the buyer's earnest and sincere intentions to buy the

property. It should be held by the attorney in a trust account or escrow account.

If the buyer completes the purchase as agreed, the earnest money payment applies as part of the purchase price. If the buyer backs out of the agreement, you *may* be entitled to the earnest money deposit for your troubles.

The earnest money payment should be large enough to make the buyer feel obligated. For example, on a $100,000 purchase, a minimum of $3,000 to $5,000 might be acceptable, although, many sellers would prefer to see a larger amount, perhaps as high as 10% of the sales price.

- A statement that the seller shall maintain insurance on the property until the date of closing for at least as much coverage as the sales price.
- A statement that you as seller must deliver good and clear title.
- An identification of the various selling costs that are to be paid by the seller and the buyer.
- Any special provisions or conditions of the sale.
- Any other terms agreed upon by the buyer and the seller.
- The date the agreement is signed.
- Signatures of the buyer(s) and the seller(s).
- The attorney may be able to suggest additional provisions that are necessary to add clarity and enforceability to your particular transaction.

All specific dates for future performance should be reasonable enough so that the required activity can be easily completed within that time frame. For instance, it will most likely take 2 to 3 weeks for the buyer to obtain a conventional loan commitment; a FHA, VA, or FmHA loan may take 4 weeks or longer. Therefore, at least this amount of time should be allowed for that performance.

Enforcing the Agreement

A written contract for the sale (or purchase) of real estate is enforceable through the use of the court system; a verbal agreement is not.

You should first of all make every attempt to assure yourself that you are dealing with a sincere buyer who will make every effort to complete the purchase as agreed. The vast majority of real estate sales contracts are performed as intended and no problem arises about the enforcement of the agreement.

State law provides several remedies to the seller if the buyer attempts to back out of the agreement after the contract is signed. If a controversy arises, you should immediately check with your attorney for advice and guidance. Before resorting to any of the legal remedies listed below, you should make every attempt to encourage the buyer to voluntarily complete the contract as agreed.

1. Sue for *specific performance*. That is, you can sue to force the buyer to complete the contract exactly as it is written.

2. Sue for monetary damages. If, as a result of the buyer's backing out, you suffered a financial loss, you can sue the buyer for that amount. For example: Assume the buyer agreed to buy your home for $100,000 and then backed out. Let us further assume that the best price you can obtain from a second buyer is $95,000. You have suffered a $5,000 loss because the first buyer failed to honor the agreement, so you can sue for the $5,000 plus other miscellaneous costs you incurred.

3. Acceptance of earnest money deposit. If the buyer backs out of the agreement, the buyer's earnest money deposit does *not* automatically become yours. Either the

buyer will have to agree to forfeit it in exchange for your releasing the buyer from the contract, or you will have to sue to get it.

4. Mutual termination of the agreement. If you sympathize with the buyer's reasons for not completing the agreement, you can simply release the buyer from any further obligation without penalty. This would put you and the buyer back to your original positions before the agreement was signed. (It should be noted that if your property is being sold by a real estate agent and you release the buyer from their contract to buy your home, you may still be obligated to pay the real estate commission, since the real estate agent did perform.)

5. No damages suffered. If the buyer's backing out of the agreement did not cause you any financial loss, you probably have no cause to expect damages. For example: If the buyer had agreed to buy your home for $100,000 but backed out and the next day you sold it for $105,000, you have suffered no loss because of the first buyer's actions.

It should be mentioned that similar remedies are available to the buyer if the seller attempts to back out of the agreement. This indicates that you (and your spouse) must be definite and certain in your intentions to sell according to the terms of the agreement before you sign the contract.

18

Steps in Closing the Sale

For all practical purposes, your involvement in the closing process of the sale of your home is limited to one thing: Show up at your attorney's office at the appointed time with your checkbook. Your attorney will take care of all of the advance legwork and paperwork for you. The attorney will then have a series of papers and checks for you to sign, or you may only sign the deed if the lawyer transfers all of the funds through a trust account.

The closing process will be effortless and painless, and you will end up with a check for your net proceeds of the sale. Most likely, your attorney will issue all checks in your behalf to pay off your loan balance and accrued interest and your other closing costs. The attorney will furnish you with a *closing statement* identifying each payment.

The buyer may or may not be at the attorney's office at the same time you are. If the buyer is there, it should be a pleasant, mutually beneficial transaction for all. Whatever you do, don't attempt to change any terms or conditions of the sale at this point. Sales have been killed at the last moment by an unwitting seller who has blurted out, "Oh by the way, that light fixture in the kitchen doesn't stay with the house," or some similar statement. If you have followed all of the suggestions in this book, you will never get into a position where a statement like that will seem necessary. (Note: If the buyer is obtaining a loan to purchase the property, all or part of the buyer's closing procedures may take place at the lender's office.)

SELLER'S PROCEDURES BEFORE CLOSING DATE

The following steps and procedures must be completed by the seller or on the seller's behalf prior to the closing date. Depending on the terms of the contract and the seller's circumstances, some of these steps may not apply to a particular sale of real estate.

- Update the abstract or furnish the appropriate alternate evidence of title.
- Complete or make satisfactory arrangements to complete any lender-required repairs.
- Complete or make satisfactory arrangement to complete any repairs or improvements to the property as required by the buyer under the sales agreement.
- Have survey completed if required by the agreement.
- Determine if your homeowner's insurance policy is assignable to the buyer and if so, determine the amount of insurance premium proration.
- Determine amount of real estate tax proration.
- Determine amount of proration for prepaid rent or other similar items.
- Give eviction notice to tenants if sales contract calls for it.
- Determine exact payoff figure required to pay off your real estate loan.

- Get any liens against the property released.
- Pay any special assessments against the property according to the terms of the agreement.
- Have the deed prepared.
- Adhere to other special provisions as stated in the sales agreement.

BUYER'S PROCEDURES BEFORE CLOSING DATE

The following must be completed by the buyer or on the buyer's behalf prior to the closing date. Depending on the terms of the agreement and the buyer's circumstances, some of these steps may not apply to a particular sale of real estate.

As the seller, you should occasionally monitor the buyer's progress in completing these steps and should provide any assistance and encouragement that you can.

- Apply for real estate loan and receive a lender's loan commitment.
- Have the property surveyed if the agreement calls for the buyer to do this.
- Arrange to assume the seller's homeowner's insurance policy, or arrange for a new policy to be effective on the date of purchase.
- Have an attorney render an opinion on the abstract or other evidence of title to determine if the seller is furnishing good and merchantable title.
- Satisfy any conditions that must be met before the sales agreement becomes effective.
- Make any arrangements necessary to accumulate sufficient down payment cash such as liquidating investments, borrowing cash value of life insurance policies, and so forth.
- After the closing, the buyer will want to record the

deed in the county courthouse as proof of ownership. If the buyer has obtained a loan, the lender will take care of this, since the lender will want to file a lien against the property at the same time.

After you have signed the deed and it has been delivered to the buyer, ownership has been transferred. You should therefore be prepared to turn the keys to the property over to the buyer at this point.

19

Vacating the Property

You must vacate the property on or before the date specified in your agreement. Ordinarily this will coincide with the closing date (the date when final settlement is made and the deed is transferred). In some cases, however, your agreement may call for your giving possession of the property before or after the closing date.

Customarily, if the buyer moves in before the closing date, the buyer will pay you rent for those days. Likewise, if you are allowed to stay in the home after the closing date, you will most likely pay the buyer rent.

SHOULD POSSESSION BE GIVEN BEFORE THE CLOSING DATE?

Many sellers prefer that the buyer not be allowed to take possession of the home before final settlement is made on the closing date. There may be several legitimate reasons for this:

1. With the purchase of almost any home, there may be a few "surprises" in store for the buyer when he or she moves in. The seller is fearful that the buyer may dis-

cover some inconsequential imperfection in the home that the buyer had not previously noticed. Because of it, the buyer may balk at completing the purchase or may make unreasonable demands upon the seller.

It's not that the seller is trying to hide anything or shirk responsibility under the agreement. It's simply that the seller is afraid that the buyer will become unnecessarily upset over some minor thing that would otherwise be overlooked if the buyer had already made payment for the home.

2. What happens if through negligence or lack of knowledge the buyer ruins the furnace, water heater, garbage disposal, air conditioner, or plumbing? Who is to pay for that?

If this occurred after the buyer had made payment (assuming these things worked properly before the buyer took possession), there would be no question about it: The buyer would have to withstand the cost of repairs. If the buyer took possession of the property before payment is made and then ruined or damaged something, however, the buyer might expect the seller to pay for the repairs.

3. If, for some reason, the buyer fails to be able to complete the purchase, problems may develop with evicting the erstwhile buyer from the premises. Even if the buyer leaves voluntarily, wear and tear or damage might be caused to the property.

LAST-MINUTE DETAILS

Your goal in vacating the property should be to leave the home in the same condition you would like it to be left for you if you were the buyer. Some of the procedures suggested below may be already required of you by your agreement with the buyer, others are for your own benefit, and others are a matter of courtesy to the buyer.

- Leave everything in excellent condition. Vacuum and shampoo carpets if necessary. Wash or dust counters and cabinet shelves, and wipe smudges from the walls.
- Leave behind any extra paint, wallpaper, and carpet that matches that in the home.
- Leave all instruction books, guarantees, and so forth in an easy-to-find place.
- Patch and touch-up paint excessive nail holes in the walls.
- Repair any appliances, light switches, etc. that do not work. Normally your contract will call for you to guarantee that all of these items are in good working condition on the closing date of the sale.
- Remove all garbage and unwanted items from the premises.
- Complete all property improvements that are required of you by the contract or by a lender.
- Double-check to see that you are leaving behind all items that are to stay with the home.
- Have a final reading of all utilities meters and have utilities disconnected or transferred to the buyer. Collect deposits you have coming from utility companies.
- Vacate the property on or before the date called for in your agreement. Lock all doors—deliver the keys to the buyer.

Leaving the property in top-notch condition will create good will with the buyer. You will never need to fear that the buyer will "bad mouth" you all over town for leaving the home in a mess. And, if there are a few inconsequential "surprises" when the buyer moves in, the buyer will have a tendency to overlook them if you have apparently tried your best to deliver the home in good condition.

20

Income Tax Consequences of Your Sale

Under some circumstances you will need to pay income taxes if you sell your home at a profit. Under other circumstances, that tax is deferred until later, or you may not have to pay income taxes at all. An understanding of the income tax consequences of your sale will help you make your future plans intelligently.

DETERMINING AMOUNT OF PROFIT ON THE SALE

The amount of profit that might be recognizeable for income tax purposes is the difference between the *cost basis* and the *adjusted sales price* of the home. Various expenditures incurred in the purchase and sale of the home are recognized in calculating these two amounts as shown below.

Calculating the Cost Basis

The cost basis of your home is the amount you paid for it, plus all closing cost fees, such as legal fees, recording fees, and so forth, and the cost of any major improvements made to the home. Major improvements would include the cost of any additions to the home (a new family room, for instance), a new air-conditioning system, a new sidewalk, or anything else that has a long-term usage. Ordinary, maintenance and repairs such as painting or replacing broken windows do not fall within this category.

For example: Assume you purchased your home several years ago at a purchase price of $60,000. Closing costs amounted to $800. Through the years you added a swimming pool, cement driveway, new central air-conditioning unit, and double garage, all at a cost of $31,000. Your cost basis of the home would therefore be $91,800 as itemized below:

Purchase price:	$60,000
Add:	
Closing costs:	800
Major improvements:	31,000
Cost basis of home:	$91,800

It should be noted that there are many expenditures that may or may not qualify as major improvements to your home, depending upon the individual circumstances. You will be well advised to keep accurate records of all expenditures. When you sell your property, you can then furnish this data to your tax accountant who will be able to calculate an accurate cost basis for your home.

If you built your home, the cost basis would include the price of the lot and the entire cost of construction. Any of your own labor or that volunteered by friends cannot be included.

Calculating the Adjusted Sales Price

To calculate the adjusted sales price, start with the sales price as shown on the sales agreement. From it, deduct all closing costs related to the sale such as legal fees, abstracting or other evidence of title, *transfer tax*, and so forth. (If you had used the services of a real estate agent, the commission charges would also be deductible.)

You can also deduct any fix-up or repair work done on the home to improve its saleability. In order to be deductible, these expenses must be incurred within 90 days preceding the date on which the sales contract is signed and must be paid for within 30 days after that date.

For example: Assume you sell your home for $120,000. Closing costs amount to $2,000 and fix-up expenses incurred within the allowable time limit are $1,000. Your adjusted sales price would be $117,000 as itemized below:

Sales price:		$120,000
Less:		
Closing costs:	$2,000	
Fix-up expenses:	1,000	
Total deductions:		3,000
Adjusted sales price:		$117,000

The use of the adjusted sales price and the cost basis is described below.

Calculating the Profit

Now that the cost basis of your home and its adjusted sales price have been determined, the amount of profit can be calculated by finding the difference as shown on the following page.

Adjusted sales price:	$117,000
Less cost basis:	91,800
Profit on sale of home:	$ 25,200

Determining If Profit Is Taxable

If you purchase or build another home as your primary residence within 24 months before or after the date of your sale that is equal to your adjusted sales price or greater, income taxes on your profit on the sale are postponed; you pay no taxes now.

For example: The adjusted sales price on the sale of your home is $117,000. If, within the time limits described above, you purchase another home or build one at a price of $117,000 or more, you will pay no income tax on the $25,200 profit realized on the sale now; it will be postponed.

You can continue to postpone recognizing the profit on each home you own and resell as long as you follow the guidelines described above each time. In all cases, to qualify for income tax postponement, the property must be your *primary* residence.

Income Tax Exclusion For Persons 55 Or Older

A person who is 55 years old or older who sells a home that has been their primary residence for 3 of the last 5 years is entitled to a once-in-a-lifetime exclusion of income taxes on the first $125,000 of *profit*, even if there is no reinvestment in another home. Income taxes must be paid on the profit exceeding $125,000.

This means that if you are near age 55 and are planning to sell your home to buy a smaller and less expensive one, it will be worthwhile to wait until you are 55 before selling your home.

Be aware that once you are involved in taking the

once-in-a-lifetime exclusion individually or with a spouse, you can never take another exclusion even if you later marry someone who has not taken this exclusion. For example: John and Marsha Woods sold their home and took advantage of the once-in-a-lifetime exclusion. John died and Marsha later married Bill Adams who owned a home and had never taken the once-in-a-lifetime exclusion. Since Marsha had been involved in taking the exclusion previously, Bill Adams is now not allowed to take the exclusion since he is married to Marsha.

DETERMINING YOUR INCOME TAXES IF YOU DO NOT REINVEST

If you sell your primary residence, do not reinvest in another home, and do not claim the over age 55 tax exclusion, *all* profit realized on the sale is taxable as *ordinary income* at your regular income tax rate. The Tax Reform Act of 1986 eliminated the long-term capital gain tax advantage previously enjoyed by sellers of real estate.

Thus, if you owned the home in the preceding example, the entire $25,200 profit would have been taxable at your regular income tax rate. Assuming a 38% rate, your income tax would then have been $9,576.

If you sell your home at a profit and then purchase a less expensive home, a portion of your profit on the sale will be taxable according to the preceding guidelines.

CHECKING CURRENT INCOME TAX REGULATIONS

Income tax regulations are subject to change each year. Even though the amounts, percentages, ages, and so forth described above are current at the time of this writing, they may soon be modified. Most likely, the general principles will remain the same, but the specifics may change.

Before you embark on the sale of your home or other real estate, you should check with your accountant to receive an explanation of current income tax regulations and how they will affect you.

21

If All Else Fails (Selecting a Real Estate Agent)

If all goes as anticipated, you won't need to read this chapter. You'll be able to carry out every step of the sale of your home without the aid of a real estate agent. However, circumstances might lead you to want or need the services of a real estate company. This might occur if you're leaving the community or if you have exhausted all of your own potential buyers.

A real estate agent should be picked very carefully. A good one will actively work on the sale of your property and will keep you informed of all progress. A poor one will be worse than having no one at all and will cause you great distress.

ANALYZING THE REAL ESTATE COMMISSION

The real estate commission paid for the sale of your home is actually divided into two portions by the real estate agents involved: the listing portion and the sales portion. This means that if your home is listed by one agent and sold by another, they will split the commission. The listing agent receives the listing portion; the selling agent receives the selling portion.

The commission split between listing portion and selling portion varies with local custom, but either 40% to the lister and 60% to the seller or a 50–50 split are common. Therefore, if a 40–60 split is used and the total commission on your property is $10,000, the lister gets $4,000; the seller gets $6,000. If the same person both lists and sells the property, they get the whole amount.

This rather lengthy description is presented to point out an extremely important aspect in selecting a real estate agent. That is, real estate agents earn far more money if they sell their own listings than if they sell another agent's listings. Because of this factor, most real estate agents place most of their emphasis on trying to sell their own listings rather than another agent's. In fact, some real estate agents virtually refuse to show another agent's listings.

This arrangement of splitting the real estate commission between the lister and the seller usually prevails between agents of the same company, or between one real estate company and another.

In choosing a real estate agent to list your property, then, it can be seen that the *one* real estate agent whom you must look to and rely on for performance is the one who listed your property. That agent has the most to gain by making the sale.

In many communities, the real estate companies offer a *multiple listing service*. Under this arrangement, each real estate company's listings are made available to all other participating companies. Any member agent can then show and sell any property listed by any participating real estate company in the community.

Some homeowners then feel that all they need to do is list their home with any member agent and then every real estate agent in the community will work on the sale of the home. In theory this is true, but in actual practice it's usually a fallacy. This is because of the reasons outlined above: Only the one agent whom you list with will feel obligated to work on the sale of your home; the others will do so only if it is convenient for them.

QUALITIES TO LOOK FOR IN A LISTING AGENT

From the preceding discussion, it can be seen that the one specific agent you choose to list your property with is the one who's most likely to put forth the best sales effort. Therefore, you must choose a listing agent based upon that person's sales abilities.

In general, you should choose the best salesperson from a top real estate company. In this way, you'll get the personal sales effort of a top person, and you'll get the advertising, promotion, and referral services of a top company.

If possible, try to identify a salesperson who performs particularly well in the type of market that currently exists in your community. That is, one salesperson might flourish in a seller's market but flounder in a buyer's market, while the opposite may be true of another salesperson.

Do not haphazardly telephone or walk into a real estate company and list your property with whoever has *floor duty* (whereby within a real estate office the salespeople take turns on who gets unsolicited customers) that day. You may end up with the agency's poorest, least productive salesperson. Instead, carefully investigate beforehand by asking around the community and handpick the agent with whom you will list your property.

Try to select an enthusiastic salesperson who personally likes your home and who thinks that they can sell it. If the salesperson seems to lack interest and enthusiasm, find someone else.

Types of Listing Agreements

Several types of listing agreements under which you can list your property are available and are shown below. Although the type of listing is negotiable between the owner and the listing real estate company, most real estate companies refuse to list a residential property under any arrangement but the *exclusive right to sell*.

Open Listing

Under an *open listing*, the owner can engage any number of real estate agents on a nonexclusive basis. The agent who sells the property gets the full commission and the rest get nothing. Also, if the owner sells his or her own property, no real estate commission is paid to any real estate agent.

This may sound like the ideal type of listing, but often it's not. First, very few real estate agencies will accept this type of listing. Second, even though all real estate agents can work on the sale of the property on an equal basis, no one is obligated to do so. Third, since the owner can sell the property, he or she is actually operating in competition with the real estate agents, which can cause major problems for both the owner and the real estate agents.

Exclusive Agency Listing

Under this arrangement, the property is listed with one real estate company, who in turn can and probably will make it available to other real estate companies. The owner also reserves the right to sell the property without payment of a real estate commission.

This type of listing has some of the same inherent problems associated with the open listing, as described above.

Exclusive Right to Sell

Under the exclusive right to sell listing, the property is listed with one specific agency, who may then make it available to other cooperating real estate companies. The listing agent gets the real estate commission regardless of who sells the property, even if it is sold by the owner. Of course, if a cooperating agency sells the property, that company receives the sales portion of the commission, and the listing agency retains the listing portion.

This listing arrangement is the type most often used and is usually the most beneficial for the owner. This is because it assures the listing agent of a commission if the property is sold. Therefore, the lister can devote time and energy to the sale of the property without the fear, as with the listings previously described, that it will all be for free.

Obviously, if the owner feels he or she can sell the property themselves, they should do so before listing it under this or any other type of listing agreement.

Net Listing

With a *net listing*, the owner is to receive a preset, specific sum for the sale of the home, say $95,000, and the real estate agent receives anything that the property is sold for above that as their commission.

This type of listing is illegal in many states and is frowned upon by the real estate commissions in most others. This is because an unscrupulous real estate agent could take unfair advantage of an unwitting home-owner.

For example: If you agree to accept $95,000 for your home and the real estate agent sells it for $115,000, the agent would receive a $20,000 commission. Rightfully, this money, less a fair real estate commission, should be yours.

On the other hand, if the property were sold for $95,000 or less, the real estate agent would receive no commission at all for their efforts. For this reason, most real estate agents are no more willing than most home-owners to utilize a net listing.

It is strongly recommended that a net listing be avoided.

Negotiating the Commission Rate

By law, the rate of real estate commission must be nego-tiated on between the property owner and the real estate agent on each individual listing. State law does not set the rate of commission, and it is a violation of *anti-trust laws* for competing real estate companies to fix real es-tate commissions at a set rate in their community.

Most real estate companies, just like barbers, bakers, gasoline service stations, and other businesses, have a set rate that they charge for their services. Most likely, the rate charged by all real estate companies in a com-munity is the same, or very similar, since competition more or less dictates what can be charged.

Still, the temptation might exist for an owner to want

to negotiate to a lower commission rate than that ordinarily charged. The question is, should you do it? Generally, the answer is *no*. This is because if you negotiate to a lower rate than your agent receives from the sale of other similar properties, you are in effect offering to pay less than others are willing to pay for the sale of their homes. Because of human nature, you might then expect that your agent might put forth his or her best efforts in trying to sell those properties where the greatest commission can be earned by them—on other properties, not yours.

It should be pointed out that if your property is unique and unusually saleable, negotiation to a lower commission rate might be appropriate. If your property is of this variety, however, you will most likely have sold it yourself by now, anyway, and the question of whether or not to negotiate to a lower commission rate will never come up.

Conversely then, is it worth paying a higher commission rate than ordinarily charged as an inducement to real estate salespeople to put forth extra effort on the sale of your home? Your attitude toward this ploy and your general circumstances should be your guide. If you are in a hurry to make the sale or are nearing the point of desperation, it may be worth considering.

LENGTH OF THE LISTING PERIOD

The length of time for which you list your property is set by agreement between the owner and the listing real estate agent. Legally, any time period is acceptable. Many real estate companies have their own policies, or they may need to follow multiple listing association guidelines pertaining to the length of listing period. Often, a minimum of 30 days is required.

Most real estate agents want as long a listing period as they can get the owner to agree to. In a strong market, where properties are selling quickly, they may seek a minimum listing of 6 months. In a tough market, where it may take longer to sell a property, they may seek a listing of a minimum of a year. This is because a long listing assures them that they will have a long period over which to work on the sale of your property, and probably within that long time period the home will sell. There is danger, however, for the homeowner in listing as long as 6 months or more. That is, if the real estate agent turns out to be ineffective or does not work on your property, you are stuck with them for a long time.

In all fairness to the listing agent, you will need to list for a long enough time to give the agent a chance to get some activity started. A 30-day listing is really too short; by the time the real estate agent gets some things started, the listing expires. Also, if the listing is for such a short duration, many real estate companies will not invest much in promoting and advertising the property since their chances of getting a return on their investment is minimized by the short listing period. You can, of course, extend the listing at the end of the 30 days, but the real estate agent has no advance assurance that you will do so.

A 3-month to 4-month listing period is recommended as being the ideal length. It gives the listing agent a sufficient amount of time to work on the sale of the property and is a long enough listing to merit advertising and promotional expenditures by the lister's company. From the owner's point of view, it ties the property up for a reasonable but not excessive time period. If the listing agent turns out to be ineffective, you don't have too long to wait until you can relist with someone else.

If the listing expires without the property being sold,

you must then make another decision. Will you list again with the same real estate agent, list with someone else, or attempt to sell the property yourself? If you decide to relist and were pleased with the efforts of your original lister, you should probably relist with them. If you were displeased, you should list with someone else, maybe someone who worked hard on the sale of the property even though it was not their listing.

DETERMINING THE LISTING PRICE

If you have attempted to sell your property yourself before listing with a real estate agent, the highest price at which you can logically list has already been set—it's the price you have been quoting. To try to raise the price is usually folly, since any prospective buyer who finds out that you were previously quoting a lower price will either avoid your property or will offer you your previous asking price or a lower one, anyway.

No doubt, you have selected a real estate agent in whom you have confidence. Rely upon that agent's professional opinion to guide you in setting the listing price. Ultimately though, since you own the property, the final decision in setting a listing price is yours. If you set a price, however, that's far beyond what your listing agent recommends, you have tied your agent's hand, since you are asking the agent to sell the property for more than the agent believes it's worth.

In all cases, list the property at a reasonable price that's within the realm of being attractive to prospective buyers.

Determining the proper listing price will probably present no consternation for you at this point if you properly appraised your property before attempting to sell it yourself. That price will still be accurate.

The Listing Agent's Duties to You

The listing agreement spells out the lister's responsibilities to you. These are probably stated in general terms and include the following:

- To diligently attempt to secure a buyer for the property.
- To furnish you with any information you request as to the agent's progress.
- To relist the property with a multiple listing association or make it available to other cooperating real estate companies.

In addition to these stipulations, the listing agent and all other real estate agents who work on the sale of the property have certain obligations to you.

1. Since you are paying the real estate commission, any real estate agent who works on the sale of the property is working for you—not the buyer. Therefore, it's your best interests that the real estate agents should be pursuing.

Only if the buyer is paying a finder's fee to a real estate agent for locating is the agent working for the buyer. This is seldom done when a buyer purchases residential property. In a situation like that, the real estate agent must reveal to you his or her dual role in this transaction.

2. The real estate agent must keep any secret information that you have divulged strictly confidential. For instance, if your home is listed at $95,000, but you have told the real estate agent that you would accept $90,000 if necessary, the agent is not to divulge that fact unless you give permission to do so.

Since some real estate agents have been known to betray an owner's trust in a situation like this, you're probably better off by not providing a real estate agent with this type of inside information.

3. Any written offers received by a real estate agent must be presented to you, even if they appear to be ridiculously low. If an offer is too low, you can reject it or counteroffer, but you must be given the chance to make that decision.

Since oral offers to buy real estate are not binding, an oral offer is in effect no offer at all. Even though that's the case, the real estate agent should still inform you of this degree of progress. If the real estate agent has an interested party but cannot get them to sign a written offer, *you* might make a written offer to sell and have your agent present it to the potential buyer. This is an unusual maneuver, but it will at least force the prospect to make a decision on your property.

4. After an agreement is signed to sell the property, the real estate agent has a responsibility to shepherd the transaction through to its completion. This includes follow-up to see that the buyer meets all requirements and completion of all paperwork connected to the sale.

5. It should be pointed out that the owner has the right to cancel a listing agreement before its expiration date if the listing agent fails to service the listing adequately. Essentially, if the listing agent has abandoned the listing by putting forth no effort or spending no time on it, a cancellation may be warranted.

If the listing agent agrees to the cancellation, have the agent sign a release. This will enable you to relist with someone else or to sell the property yourself. If the listing agent does not agree to the cancellation, your only remedy is to resort to the courts, which may not be worth your time, effort, and cost.

Your Duties to the Listing Agent

The listing agreement sets forth your responsibilities to the listing agent and most likely will include the following:

1. To allow the showing of the property at all reasonable times.
2. To refer to the listing agent any inquiries about the property by prospective buyers.

If the real estate company places a lawn sign in front of your home, identifying that it is for sale, an occasional passerby may stop in on their own to view your home. If they do, get their name, address, and telephone number and relay it to your listing agent. If it's not awkward to do so, call the lister immediately in the hope that the agent can rush to your home to make the showing.

Since your listing agreement will probably be an exclusive right to sell listing, the listing agent receives the commission even if you sell the property yourself. Therefore, you should involve the lister as completely as you can with any prospects that you come up with by yourself.

3. Payment of the agreed-upon real estate commission on the sale of the property.

Listing agreements ordinarily contain a *protective clause* that states that if the property is sold by the real estate agent or by the owner within a specific time (often 6 months) after the listing expires, to a prospect who was introduced to the property during the listing period, the real estate agent still receives the agreed-upon commission. The purpose of this clause is to prohibit the owner from dealing on the sale of the property behind the agent's back to the detriment of the agent.

To enforce this clause, the real estate agent must furnish the owner with a written list of prospects, who qualify under this provision, before the listing agreement expires.

The owner is also responsible for paying the commission if the real estate agent submits an offer at the seller's price and terms that is turned down by the owner. This is because the real estate agent has performed according to the provisions of the listing agreement and should therefore be compensated. This indicates that an owner should be certain that he or she intends to sell their property before they sign a listing agreement.

In addition to these provisions contained in the listing agreement, there are other steps that you can take to assist in making the property more saleable and to help in making the listing agent's job easier.

1. If you tried to sell your home yourself, you most likely have many names of potential buyers. Turn these over to your listing agent. Even though you were unable to get a prospect to buy, perhaps the real estate salesperson can.

Even if one of these prospects buys a home other than yours, it may free up someone down the line who will buy your home. Also, the real estate agent will feel indebted to you because of your fine cooperation and will most likely put forth extra effort on the sale of your home.

2. Keep your listing agent informed of any changes in your or your home's status. If you have made changes or improvements to the property, must change the possession date, or have decided to include or exclude additional items, update your agent.

3. If you'll be gone from the home over the weekend or on vacation, inform your agent where you'll be and how you can be contacted. If you have not already provided one, leave a key to your home with your agent.

Keeping in Touch With the Listing Agent

Any active real estate agent has many clients to whom they owe a responsibility. Often they operate under the "If you don't hear from me, it's because I have nothing to report" philosophy. Therefore, if you want to know what activity is taking place on your property, you may need to contact your listing agent.

Contacting your listing agent every two weeks or so is probably a good idea. It periodically reminds the agent of your property and more or less places the agent on the spot to produce some results, the "Squeaky wheel gets the grease" theory.

Your attitude and approach in contacting your agent is important. Ideally, you should call to deliver the name of a prospect you have uncovered or to provide updated information on your circumstances. Of course, you'll want to ask what progress is being made on the sale of your home.

Don't become rude, overbearing, insulting, demanding, accusing, or critical in your conversation. It will only cause your agent to want nothing to do with you and to "hide" from you. Instead, be understanding and encouraging. Your agent will appreciate your attitude and will put forth a better effort for you.

22

Getting Started

All of the techniques presented in this book will be of no value to you unless you use them. Don't attempt to attack all phases of selling your home at once. Break the procedure into logical steps and work at it methodically.

Expect that selling your own home will occupy some of your time—but it will be worth it. If you devote 10 hours a week to this project for 5 weeks and save $5,000 in real estate commissions, you will have earned $100 per hour for your efforts! Of course, no one can project how long it will take to sell your home, but one thing can be projected: You *can* sell your own home if you work at it, even in a difficult economic climate!

You're about to undertake one of the most exciting, rewarding, and profitable ventures of your life—selling your own home. Don't worry, don't wait, don't tary, don't hesitate—the time to get started is *now*. Good Luck!

Glossary of Real Estate Terms*

Abstract of title: A brief history of title to a tract of real estate that shows all transfers and encumbrances (liens, etc.) pertaining to the property.

Acceleration clause: A clause in a loan agreement that states that the lender can call the entire remaining loan due if the borrower fails to make a scheduled loan payment or meet some other requirement.

Accrued interest: Interest that has accumulated on a loan since the last loan payment was made.

Ad valorem tax: The general real estate tax levied against property according to its value.

Adjustable-rate mortgage: A type of real estate loan that allows the lender to raise (or lower) the interest rate on existing loans if current interest rates rise (or decrease).

Adjusted net income: A term used with Farmer's Home Administration (FmHA) loans to identify the income level applicants must meet to qualify for a loan.

Adjusted sales price: The difference between the sales price and the cost basis of a home.

* NOTE: Not all of the terms presented here are included in the text of this book.

Adverse possession: A statutory procedure whereby one person can acquire title to another's property by the open, hostile, notorious, exclusive use of the property for a time period set by state statute.

Agent (real estate): A real estate broker who works on behalf of a person, known as the *principal*, to accomplish a specific act, usually involved in the sale or purchase of real estate.

Agreement: Another term used to identify a contract between two or more parties.

Air rights: The space above land which often has value, particularly in urban areas.

Alienation clause: The clause in a loan agreement that states that the remaining balance of the loan becomes due and payable if the borrower sells the property.

Anti-trust laws: Laws that prohibit agreements between businesses that will have the effect of limiting or eliminating competition.

Appraisal: An estimate of the value of real property.

Appreciation: The increase in value of property over a period of time, often caused by prolonged inflation.

Asking price: The price that a seller quotes as the amount that they want for the property.

Assessment (general real estate tax): The determining of a property's value and the application of a tax rate to that value by a County Assessor to determine the real estate taxes on the property.

Assessment (special): A tax levy against specific real estate for street repairs, storm sewer, etc. that benefits that particular property.

Assets: Anything of value that is owned.

Assumption (of loan): Whereby the buyer takes over the seller's existing loan at a lending institution and assumes all future responsibility for the loan payments.

Balance sheet: A form that lists a person's or company's assets, liabilities, and net worth.

Balloon payment: The lump sum payment of a remaining loan balance, usually made at the end of a period over which periodic payments have been made.

Breach of contract: The failure of a party to a contract to adhere to the contract's terms.

Broker (real estate): A person who works for another as an agent in the buying and selling of real estate.

Building code: Regulations, usually local in nature, that specify procedures and materials to be used in the construction of homes and other structures.

Buyer's market: Sluggish market conditions where sellers outnumber buyers and buyers may get a good buy.

Carpet allowance: Whereby a home seller pays the buyer a certain amount that the buyer can use to recarpet the property with carpet of the buyer's own choosing.

Cash sale: A sale of real estate whereby the buyer pays cash and does not rely upon funds from a lending institution.

Cash value, life insurance: The value of a permanent life insurance policy that the policy owner can borrow or take in cash if the policy is cancelled. Borrowing the cash value is often an excellent way for a buyer to secure down payment money.

Caveat emptor: A Latin term that means "Let the buyer beware." In real estate transactions, this indicates that the buyer must make note of obvious property defects when viewing the property.

Character: A general description of a person's quality and reputation that is weighed by a lender when contemplating making a loan to an applicant.

Closing statement: A written statement provided to the seller by the attorney or real estate agent handling the details of the sale, showing all cash receipts and disbursements. A similar statement is furnished to the buyer.

Commission rate: A percentage rate of commission charged by a real estate broker. This rate is applied to the full sales price, ordinarily, to determine the amount of real estate commission.

Comparables: Properties that have similar qualities to the seller's, and which are used as a basis of comparison when appraising the seller's property.

Condominium: A form of ownership whereby a person owns an apartment in a complex or apartment building. The condominium owner also owns a share of the common elements such as the land, roof, hallways, elevators, and so forth.

Consideration: That thing of value which a party gives or receives when entering into a contract. In a real estate transaction, consideration is often the giving of a house and land on one hand for the receipt of money on the other.

Contract: An agreement entered into between two or more competent parties. To be enforceable, contracts for the sale of real estate must be in writing.

Contract for deed: An arrangement for the sale of real estate under which the buyer takes possession of the property, makes periodic payments to the seller, and the seller retains actual title to the property until it is paid for in full by the buyer.

Conventional loan: The "regular" type of real estate loan made by Savings and Loan Associations, Mutual Savings Banks, and commercial banks. Ordinarily, a down payment of at least 20% of the purchase price is required of the buyer.

Cooperative (housing): A form of ownership whereby a person "owns" an apartment in a complex or apartment building. The owner does not actually receive title to the apartment unit, but rather, receives shares of stock in the cooperative association that owns all of the apartment units in the complex and receives a proprietary lease to the specific apartment unit occupied.

Cost basis: The amount paid for a home plus all closing cost fees, recording fees, and so forth, and the cost of any major improvements to the property. This is subtracted from the adjusted sales price when the property is sold to determine the amount of profit on the sale.

Cost plus inflation: A method of determining real estate market value by starting with the owner's cost and adding the estimated inflation rate for each year the property was owned. This may not give an exact market value figure, but it will give an approximation.

Counteroffer: Ordinarily, the prospective buyer makes an offer to the seller of real estate. If this offer is unacceptable, the seller can reject it and make a new offer to the buyer. This offer from the seller to the buyer is called a counteroffer.

County Assessor: The county official who has the responsibility to determine property values for real estate tax purposes.

County Recorder: The county official who has the responsibility to record and maintain all official records in the county. All real estate transactions are filed with the County Recorder.

Credit report: A report showing a person's borrowing and repayment record. This is of great importance to a lending institution that is contemplating making a real estate loan to a prospective borrower.

Curtsey: An ownership right granted by state law to a husband in his deceased wife's real estate. Many states have replaced the right of curtsey with an ownership right granted by statute, which does essentially the same thing.

Deed: The document that transfers ownership of real estate from one person to another.

Deed restrictions: Provisions placed in the deed by the seller that limit in some way the buyer's and all subsequent owners' use of the property. This is often done by a housing developer to create conformity of use of the property in the development.

Default: The failure of a person to carry out their obligations under a contract as required.

Deficiency judgment: If a borrower defaults on his or her loan payment, and the lender forecloses on the property, and sells it for less than the remaining loan balance, the lender may then obtain a judgment against the borrower for the remaining unpaid balance.

Delinquent taxes: Real estate taxes that have not been paid when they are due.

Discount points: A cash payment required by a lender at the time a loan is granted to compensate for making a loan at an interest rate that is lower than current rates on conventional loans. Discount points are ordinarily assessed when a borrower obtains a Federal Housing Administration (FHA) or Veteran's Administration (VA) loan. Each discount point represents one percentage point, and the amount of cash due is calculated by multiplying the number of discount points times the amount of the loan.

Documentary fee: The tax that must be paid on the transfer of real estate at the time the deed is recorded in the county courthouse. This tax is also referred to as a *transfer tax* or *revenue stamps*.

Dower: A ownership right granted by state law to a wife in her deceased husband's real estate. Many states have replaced the right of dower with an ownership right granted by statute, which does essentially the same thing.

Down payment: The amount of cash the buyer applies toward the purchase price of the property.

Dual agency: When a real estate agent acts for both the buyer and the seller at the same time in a single transaction. This can easily result in a conflict of interests, and the agent must therefore divulge his or her true positions to all parties and must receive permission to be able to continue in this role.

Due on sale clause: A stipulation in a loan agreement that states the loan must be paid off before the owner can sell the property.

Earnest money: A cash payment made by the buyer at the time a contract to buy real estate is signed that demonstrates the buyer's earnest and sincere intentions to buy the property. The earnest money deposit is ordinarily held in a lawyer's or real estate agent's trust account or escrow account until the transaction is completed.

Easement: The right to cross the land of another person, often granted to utility companies so that they can install poles and wires, or granted to a neighbor who must cross adjacent land to gain access to their own property.

Eminent domain: The right that government units, such as the federal government, state, county, or city, have to appropriate private property for public use. This is often exercised when a road is built or rerouted, or when a public facility such as a park is being developed.

Encumbrance: Any burden or claim against a property such as a lien, judgment, or easement.

Enroachment: When a building, tree, or something else improperly extends beyond an owner's lot line onto an adjoining property.

Equity: The amount of net worth, stated in dollar terms, that an owner has in a piece of property. This is the difference between the property's market value and the owner's existing loan(s) against the property.

Escrow account: An account utilized by an attorney or real estate agent for accumulating buyer's and seller's funds for the closing of a real estate transaction, or for other purposes. Escrow accounts are also used by lenders to accumulate a portion of a borrower's monthly payment for the purpose of paying real estate taxes and/or homeowner's insurance premiums on the borrower's behalf sometime in the future.

Evidence of title: Proof furnished by a seller that demonstrates that he or she has good title to a property being sold. Abstract continuation, title insurance, or the Torrens system are common evidences of title.

Exchange: Whereby owners trade properties with each other. Often, the properties are not of equal value and one party must pay the difference to the other.

Exclusive agency listing: A type of real estate listing agreement whereby the property is listed with a specific real estate agent, but the owner reserves the right to sell the property without the payment of any commission.

Exclusive right to sell listing: A type of real estate listing agreement whereby the property is listed with one specific agent who gets the real estate commission regardless of who sells the property, even if it is sold by the owner. If a cooperating agency sells the property, that company receives the sales portion of the commission, and the listing agency receives the listing portion.

Farmers Home Administration (FmHA) loan: An agency of the U.S. Department of Agriculture that makes direct loans to low- and medium-income borrowers. These loans are for property located in rural areas or in communities of 20,000 or less located outside of urban areas.

Federal Housing Administration (FHA) loans: Loans that are made by local lenders and insured by the Federal Housing Administration. FHA sets the interest rate, which is usually lower than that charged by lenders for conventional loans, so the lender ordinarily assesses discount points when granting an FHA loan.

Fee simple estate: The highest degree of ownership one can have in real property; it is full, complete ownership. It is also referred to as *fee* or *fee simple absolute*.

Fiduciary relationship: The duty of trust and confidentiality owed by a real estate agent or attorney to the buyer or seller for whom they are working.

First right of refusal: A right granted to a prospective buyer that gives them first chance to purchase property, or to match other offers, before the property is sold to someone else.

Fixtures: Items that were once personal property but have now become affixed to a house or land so that they are classified as real estate. Examples include a furnace, water heater, and light fixtures.

Foreclosure: The procedure allowed by state law whereby a lender may take steps to gain title to property on which a borrower has failed to make loan payments as agreed.

Funding Fee: A fee of 1% of the loan amount charged veterans obtaining a Veterans Administration-guaranteed loan.

Income approach, appraising: A method used in appraising investment property whereby the amount of income produced by the property is used to determine the property's market value. This method is often used for appraising rental properties like apartment complexes.

Income tax exclusion: A once-in-a-lifetime opportunity available to persons 55 years old or older who sell a home that has been their primary residence for 3 of the last 5 years. Even if there is no reinvestment in another home, the first $125,000 of profit is free from income taxes.

Installment sale: Under this basis, also called *contract for deed*, the buyer ordinarily makes a down payment on the sale closing date and then makes monthly, quarterly, semi-annual, or annual payments directly to the seller over some time period, usually several years at least.

Joint tenancy: A form of ownership of real estate or other property by two or more persons under which if one of the joint owners dies, his or her share goes to the remaining joint owners. Husbands and wives often hold property as joint tenants.

Lease: An agreement whereby one party, known as the tenant or lessee, occupies the property of another, known as the landlord or lessor, under certain stipulations agreed by the parties. A lease may be verbal or written, but a lease for more than a year must be in writing to be enforceable through the courts.

Lease-purchase: Under this arrangement to purchase property, the buyer takes possession of the home, moves in, and pays rent under a lease arrangement for a limited period, usually 6–18 months. At the end of the lease period, the buyer must purchase the property and make final settlement on the purchase price.

Leverage: An investment principle of getting maximum usage of your money by making a small down payment and borrowing as much as possible. This conserves the borrower's personal funds and makes as much use of other persons' money as possible.

Liabilities: Amounts owed to others; debts.

Lien: The right of a creditor (someone to whom you owe money) to collect amounts owed them from the proceeds of the sale of the debtor's property. If the debt is not paid, the lien holder can force the sale of the property to satisfy the debt.

Listing agreement: The contract between a property owner and a real estate agent giving the agent the authority to work on the sale of the owner's property. The listing agreement specifies the rights and responsibilities of both parties. To be enforceable, a listing agreement must be in writing.

Listing period: The length of time stated in a listing agreement for which the real estate agent is engaged to work on the sale of the owner's property. The listing may be for any time period and must expire on a definite date.

Listing price: The price at which an owner's property is offered for sale as shown on a listing agreement. Real estate agents may not quote any other price than the listing price to prospective buyers.

Loan-origination fee: A fee charged to borrowers by lenders to cover the lender's cost of establishing the loan. The amount may vary, but 1% of the amount borrowed is common.

Market value: The price a property should bring if it is placed on the market for a reasonable length of time and is given proper exposure and promotion.

Mechanic's lien: A lien on property obtained by a carpenter, contractor, carpet layer, plumber, electrician, or other tradesman for labor and/or materials provided to the property.

Metes and bounds: A method of establishing a legal description of property that describes a beginning point and directions and distances of the property lines that enclose the property, ending at the point of beginning. This method is used in nearly half of the states, most of which are in the eastern part of the United States.

Mill: Real estate tax levies are often stated in terms of mills. A mill is $1/10$ of a cent; or stated as a decimal, .001. The mill levy is multiplied times the property's assessed value to determine the amount of real estate tax due. For example, if the property is assessed at $60,000 and the tax rate is 25 mills, the amount of real estate tax due is $1,500 ($60,000 × .025 = $1,500).

Mineral rights: The right of ownership to the subsurface (below ground level). Mineral rights may have great value in oil-, gas- or mineral-producing areas. The mineral rights may be sold separately from the surface or may be leased. In residential sales, mineral rights ordinarily have no particular value and are routinely transferred with the sale of the property.

Mortgage: The pledge of real estate by a borrower as security for a loan obtained from a lender. The lender will obtain a mortgage lien on the property.

Mortgagee: A lender who makes a loan to a buyer and who subsequently receives a mortgage lien on the property.

Mortgagor: A property buyer who borrows money from a lender and who pledges the property as security for the loan.

Multiple listing service: A voluntary association of real estate companies within a community whereby each participating company's listings are made available to all other participating companies. Any member agent can then show and sell any property listed with a real estate company that is a member of the multiple listing service.

Net lease: A lease arrangement whereby the tenant pays the landlord a lease amount and also assumes responsibility for

paying the real estate taxes, insurance, and possibly maintenance and repairs on the leased property.

Net listing: Under this type of listing agreement, the owner is
to receive a preset, specific sum for the sale of the property,
and the real estate agent receives anything that the property
is sold for above that amount as his or her commission. This
type of listing is illegal in many states and is frowned upon
by the real estate commissions in most others.

Net worth: The difference between a person's assets and
liabilities—that is, the difference between all that is owned
and all that is owed. Net worth is often referred to as *capital*.

Open listing: A listing arrangement under which the owner
can engage any number of real estate agents on a nonexclusive basis. The agent who sells the property gets the full
commission and the rest get nothing. Also, if the owner sells
the property, no real estate commission is paid to any real
estate agent.

Option: An arrangement under which a property owner
(called the optioner) gives a prospective buyer (called the
optionee) the opportunity to buy the property at a stated
price within a specified time period. The prospective buyer
pays a sum of money, as agreed upon by the parties, to the
owner for keeping the offer open at that price for that time
period. If the buyer completes the purchase, the money applies to the purchase. If the prospective buyer decides not to
purchase the property, the owner keeps the money depos-
ited as payment for holding the property available under
the terms of the option agreement. An option can also be
used for the proposed lease of property.

Ordinary income: All income earned from regular sources
such as salary, wages, interest, and so forth that are taxed at
the regular income tax rate. Any profit from the sale of real
estate is taxed as ordinary income.

Percentage lease: A lease arrangement often used with commercial properties whereby the tenant's lease payment is
based on a percentage of the tenant's gross sales. The lease
arrangement often calls for a fixed payment plus a percentage of the sales over a specific amount.

Personal property: Any property that is moveable and is not attached to real estate. These items are not included in the sale of real estate unless they are specifically identified as staying with the property.

Police power: The authority of a federal, state, county, or city government unit to establish and enforce rules and regulations for the use of real estate. These often take the form of building codes, zoning regulations, and health and safety restrictions.

Possession date: The date specified in a real estate sales agreement that the buyer is to take actual possession of the property. This usually coincides with the closing date, when payment is made and title is transferred, but it is possible for the possession date to be before or after the closing date.

Prepayment penalty: A clause in a loan agreement that states that if a borrower pays off the loan before its maturity, the borrower *may* be assessed a penalty. This penalty varies, but 1% to 1½% of the remaining loan balance is a common range. Even though lenders are entitled to charge this penalty, many do not.

Primary residence: A person's principle residence, which is occupied more than 6 months of the year.

Protective clause: A clause ordinarily included in a real estate listing agreement that states that if the property is sold by the real estate agent or by the owner within a specified time (often 6 months) after the listing expires, to a prospect who was introduced to the property during the listing period, the real estate agent still receives the agreed-upon commission. To enforce this clause, the real estate agent must furnish the owner with a written list of prospects who qualify under this provision, before the listing agreement expires.

Purchase money mortgage: An arrangement under which the seller accepts a promissory note from the buyer for a portion of the purchase price.

Quitclaim deed: A deed that transfers whatever degree of ownership interest the grantor (seller, or signer) has in the property without making any warranties.

Real estate: Land and all that is permanently attached to the land including house, other buildings, fences, trees and other plantings, and all fixtures.

Real estate commission: The amount charged by a real estate agent for selling an owner's property. The commission is usually stated as a percentage of the sales price, but other arrangements, such as a flat amount, may be charged.

Real estate tax proration: Allocating real estate taxes on the property being sold to coincide with the closing date. Since real estate taxes are paid in arrears (after the tax is assessed to the property), the seller must bring the taxes up to date for the entire time period the seller had possession of the property. This requires the seller to make a payment, in the amount of those real estate taxes, to the buyer on the closing date.

Recording fees: A fee charged for recording the deed or contract for deed in the county courthouse. This is the buyer's responsibility.

Rectangular survey system: A method of surveying property and formulating a legal description that utilizes reference to meridians and base lines that are established throughout the country. A legal description for an 80-acre parcel of land using the rectangular survey system would be as follows: "The N ½ of the NE ¼ of Section 6, Township 8 North, Range 6 West of the 2nd Principal Meridian."

Redemption period: A time period, as provided by state law, during which an owner can regain possession of their property that has been foreclosed upon.

Renegotiatiable-rate mortgage: A type of real estate loan that allows the lender to raise the interest rate on existing loans if current interest rates rise.

Repairs, lender-required: Repairs and improvements that a lender requires be made to the property before the lender will extend a loan to the buyer. Often these repairs must be paid for by the seller. Federal Housing Administration-insured loans, Veteran's Administration guaranteed-loans, and Farmers Home Administration loans often require that repairs and improvements be made to the property.

Replacement cost: An appraisal method whereby the cost of rebuilding the same home at the same location at today's costs is calculated.

Revenue stamps: The tax that must be paid on the transfer of real estate at the time the deed is recorded in the courthouse. This tax is also referred to as a *transfer tax* or *documentary fee*.

Section: A square parcel of land, measuring one mile on each side, which contains 640 acres.

Security deposit: A deposit of money ordinarily required of a tenant by a landlord to defray damage to the property caused by the tenant, or to offset any unpaid rent by the tenant.

Seller's market: A strong real estate market with high buyer demand where homes may sell quickly and at good prices.

Specific performance: A legal remedy available to buyers and sellers of real estate whereby a party who fails to perform as agreed can be forced to perform exactly as the contract terms state.

Statute of Frauds: That law that states certain contracts must be in writing to be enforceable. This includes contracts for the sale of real estate, listing agreements, and leases for more than a year.

Street appearance: The appeal of a home as one views it from the outside, "standing on the street."

Strong market: A market where economic conditions are favorable and homes sell readily and at good prices.

Survey: The process of measuring and describing land to determine its location, boundaries, size, and legal description.

Tenancy in common: A form of ownership of real estate or other property by two or more persons under which if one of the joint owners dies, his or her share goes to their heirs rather than to the surviving joint owners.

Tenant: One who rents or leases property from another, known as the landlord. A tenant is also called a *lessee*.

Title insurance: An insurance policy that insures the owner from loss due to defects in the title to the property.

Torrens system: An evidence of title used in some states whereby a registration is filed with the county courthouse showing all information pertaining to the property's title and liens against the property.

Tough market: A "sluggish," "soft," or "Buyer's market" where poor market conditions make it more difficult to sell a home quickly and at a good price.

Township: A square parcel of land measuring 6 miles on each side. A township contains 36 square miles, 36 sections, and 23,040 acres.

Trade fixture: A fixture that is installed in a commercial building by a tenant for the purpose of conducting business. When the lease expires and the tenant vacates the property, the tenant is allowed to remove these trade fixtures. If damage was caused to the building by the installation or removal, the tenant must repair it.

Transfer tax: The tax that must be paid on the transfer of real estate at the time the deed is recorded in the county courthouse. This tax is also referred to as a *documentary fee* or as *revenue stamps*.

Trust account: An account maintained by an attorney or real estate agent through which a client's funds are transferred when closing a real estate transaction.

Usury: The illegal practice of charging a higher rate of interest than that allowed by law.

Variable-rate mortgage: A type of real estate loan that allows the lender to raise the interest rate on existing loans if current interest rates rise.

Variance (zoning): Obtaining permission from the county or city zoning commission to use a property for a purpose ordinarily not allowed under zoning ordinances.

Veteran's Administration loan: A real estate loan that is made by a local lender and guaranteed by the Veteran's Administration. The Veteran's Administration sets the interest rate, which is usually lower than that charged by lenders for conventional loans, so the lender ordinarily assesses discount points when granting a VA-guaranteed loan.

Warranty deed: A type of deed that transfers title to real estate under which the seller warrants that he or she is the owner, has a right to sell the property, and will protect the buyer (legally) from any claims against the property by other persons. This is the most attractive type of deed for a buyer to receive transfer of title to real estate. Most buyers insist that the seller transfer title by use of a warranty deed, also called a *general warranty deed*.

Zoning ordinance: Regulations instituted by counties and cities to regulate the type of property that can be located in specified areas and to regulate the use of property so that conformity is achieved within the community. Zoning classifications of *residential, commercial, light industrial, heavy industrial,* and *special purpose* are common.

Index